What People Are

Pagan Portals

A fascinating historical dive into a god only recently equated with the Autumn Equinox, this book is a must for those looking to deepen their scholarly research of Celtic myths, legends, and ancient practices. Balancing the academic and the practical, these pages shed light on the mysterious origins of the deity and festival called Mabon.
Raven Digitalis, author of *The Empath's Oracle* and *The Gothic Witch's Oracle*

Modern Pagans are most likely to know Mabon as a name given to the autumn equinox. This book takes us into the myths of the Welsh God Mabon – a fascinating figure who deserves to be better known and understood. Highly recommended for anyone on the Druid path.
Nimue Brown, Druid and author of *Druidry and the Ancestors*

Pagan Portals
Mabon

Discovering the Celtic God of Hunting,
Healing and Harp

Also by This Author

Pagan Portals – Modron
Meeting the Celtic Mother goddess

978-1-80341-718-9 (Paperback)
978-1-80341-734-9 (e-book)

Pagan Portals
Mabon

Discovering the Celtic God of Hunting, Healing and Harp

Kelle BanDea

MOON
BOOKS
London, UK
Washington, DC, USA

CollectiveInk

First published by Moon Books, 2025
Moon Books is an imprint of Collective Ink Ltd.,
Unit 11, Shepperton House, 89 Shepperton Road, London, N1 3DF
office@collectiveinkbooks.com
www.collectiveinkbooks.com
www.moon-books.net

For distributor details and how to order please visit the 'Ordering' section on our website.

Text copyright: Kelle BanDea 2024

ISBN: 978 1 80341 749 3
978 1 80341 871 1 (ebook)
Library of Congress Control Number: 2024937846

A CIP catalogue record for this book is available from the British Library.

Design: Lapiz Digital Services

UK: Printed and bound by 4edge Limited
Printed in North America by CPI GPS partners

We operate a distinctive and ethical publishing philosophy in all areas of our business, from our global network of authors to production and worldwide distribution.

Contents

Contents

Introduction

The Son of the Mother

Who or what is Mabon? A Sun God, born at the Winter Solstice? Or the neopagan name for the Autumn Equinox? The truth is, neither. Or at least, not quite.

Thanks to the work of prominent scholars in Brythonic Celtic material, such as the collection of medieval Welsh tales known as the *Mabinogi*, we now know a lot more about this enigmatic deity/Otherworldly figure and his myths. While the two ideas above can be and often are linked to him, they are largely a result of modern neopagan thinking and practice, which while a rich tradition in its own right, may sometimes obscure the actual history and mythology of this fascinating god, who is so much more than simply the son of a goddess.

Commonly referred to as Mabon ap Modron, his name simply means '(Great) Son of the (Great) Mother,' which makes him sound more like an archetype than a deity, and provides a perfect, if not quite blank, slate onto which to project modern ideas about him. While working with gods in neopagan practice is an individual, subjective experience, when one is working with a deity that has a known history and myth, especially when that deity comes from a historically colonized culture, I believe it is important to learn what we can about them and incorporate this into our understanding. This can only enrich and deepen our practice, and for those working with 'Celtic paganism' due to an ethnic link or because they live in what is now termed 'the Celtic fringe' (Ireland, Scotland, Wales, Cornwall and the Brythonic North of England) it can provide a powerful connection to our ancestors and/or our place.

I briefly introduced Mabon and his place in the Brythonic Celtic tradition in my first book for the Pagan Portals series;

Modron; Meeting the Celtic Mother Goddess. As the title suggests, it concentrates on Modron and her own myths and worship, which in spite of Mabon's epithet are generally quite separate. In Mabon's myth, Modron is only briefly mentioned as his mother, and so while they are often seen as two halves of a whole – and certainly can archetypally be viewed and worked with this way – they can also be studied and worked with separately. Mabon is a fascinating figure in his own right. In *Modron* he is mentioned sparingly, although he undoubtedly lurks between the lines.

In the end, I just couldn't ignore him! While you do not need to have read that book to understand this one, this work does build and expand on what I've written there, providing a deep dive into some of the ideas introduced and the stories about Mabon that are briefly mentioned.

We will begin by taking a look at the most well-known source that we have for Mabon – the tale of *Culhwch and Olwen* in the *Mabinogi* – before looking at other Welsh texts that mention him, and asking whether he serves as a template for other Welsh and Brythonic stories about sons and their mothers. I will then discuss the widespread cult of his forerunner, the god Maponus, who was worshiped as a deity in Roman Britain and Gaul, as well as taking a brief look at associated deities. With this history established, each chapter will then take a closer look at one of Mabon's primary attributes; Chapters 3 and 4 will look more deeply into his story in *Culhwch and Olwen,* examining his role as a hunter and the animals associated with him respectively, and ask just how ancient these motifs may be (spoiler; the answer is very). Chapter 3 also has a brief discussion of 'Celtic shamanism' and offers a guided journey that you may wish to try. We will then examine his epithet as an 'Exalted Prisoner' before looking at his title of 'Divine Youth' and related Celtic figures.

I believe that Mabon still has much to offer us as neopagans and spiritual practitioners in the present day, and so the book will finish with a chapter on working with him in your ritual practice, if you have one. We will also have that much needed discussion about the Autumn Equinox!

When I started writing *Modron* after a period of dedicating myself to this Mother Goddess of the Celts, I wasn't anticipating working on a companion volume about her son. I have always been more interested in female deities than male ones, having undertaken academic study into feminist theology and Goddess Studies, and have had my fill of both hyper-masculine gods and hero-kings. But the more I researched Modron herself, the more I found out about her son, and realized that he may offer something very different to what I had expected. Now, he has a regular place on my altar – and in my heart. I hope this book helps you to discover more about him, uncover him from underneath his modern gloss, and encourages you to get to know him.

Blessed be.

Chapter 1

The Tales of Mabon ap Modron

The *Mabinogi* is a collection of medieval Welsh stories with mythological motifs which point to a far older origin. They are believed to have originally been told orally, and bring together echoes of older Brythonic deities and ideas about the Otherworld in a way that has inspired neopagans, especially those working in the Celtic tradition, ever since.

Originally compiled and translated by Lady Charlotte Guest in 1838-49, the *Mabinogi* has been translated and interpreted many times since, and remains a beloved and living text. It is here that we meet Rhiannon, venerated today as a horse goddess, the shapeshifter Lleu Llaw Gyffes and his magician uncle Gwydion, the giant Bran the Blessed and his magical cauldron, and even King Arthur and his knights (although they are more of a warband than chivalrous knights at this point.) The first four tales are somewhat linked and are often referred to as the 'Four Branches,' and are of a somewhat different character to the rest of the stories, which are largely a collection of folktales and Arthurian stories.

We meet Mabon not in the Four Branches themselves but in the tale of *Culhwch and Olwen*, which is possibly the oldest tale featuring Arthur that we have so far. It is long, almost ridiculously detailed in parts, with pages devoted to roll calls of names that have led some scholars to theorize that parts of the tale were designed to be either satire, or a teaching tale for bards in training to remember the various characters in the stories they had to learn. It is almost certainly meant to be performed, not read, at least in parts. It is also something of a mash-up, being made up of pieces of separate tales that are likely to be far older than other sections of the story. The tale of the search for

Mabon may be one of the oldest parts of all, originally a more detailed myth of its own. He is not the hero of the tale by any means, and yet it cannot be told without him.

My following summary draws on Sioned Davies' translation.

Culhwch has been given a list of tasks by his prospective father-in-law, the fearsome giant Ysbaddaden, which he must complete if he is to win Olwen's hand in marriage. Many of these tasks relate to the hunting of a huge white boar known as the Twrch Trwyth, in order to acquire the comb, razor and shears that lie between his ears, in order that Ysbaddaden can dress his beard. To hunt the boar, the dog Drudwyn is required. But only one huntsman in the world can handle the hound, and he is Mabon son of Modron. But Mabon 'was taken when three nights old from his mother. No one knows where he is, nor what state he's in, whether dead or alive.' Mabon's kinsman will need to join the search for him, and Mabon also will require the great white horse Gwyn Myngddwn (as swift as a wave) who will not come willingly. Culhwch then seeks the help of the famous Arthur and his warriors (there was no round table in these early tales, nor much in the way of later medieval chivalry). Arthur's men decide to make seeking Mabon their first task. But finding him is not easy. They have to ask a sequence of ancient animals, beginning with the Blackbird of Cilgwri. Each time, the question is the same; 'For God's sake, do you know anything of Mabon son of Modron, who was taken when three nights old from between his mother and the wall?' Each animal answers with a poetic explanation of how ancient they are, before admitting that they have no idea where Mabon is, and sending the warriors to an animal who is older still; they ask first the blackbird, then a stag, then an owl, an eagle and finally a great salmon. The Salmon of Llyn Lliw gives them their answer; Mabon is imprisoned near Caerloyw

2

(on the river Severn in Gloucester) where he sits and laments his incarceration. The salmon takes Cai and Bedwyr down the river on his back while Arthur and the rest of his men attack the fort where Mabon is being held. Cai goes through the back wall and carries Mabon out on his back, finally freeing him. After various other adventures, the hunt for the Twrch Trwyth begins, but the boar proves hard to capture, and many of the men are killed. After a long adventure that sees them chase the boar from Ireland all the way to the river Severn, Mabon enters the story again, and manages to take the razor from between the animal's ears. Mabon then disappears from the narrative, but the boar is finally caught, the task completed, and Culhwch marries Olwen.

This tale provides us with our best source for the mythos of Mabon ap Modron. I will explore later in this book his role in the tale in more depth, and what it potentially reveals about him, but for now, let's look at his relation to the rest of the *Mabinogi* itself.

Mabon as Archetype

His title as 'ap Modron,' stressing his relationship to his mother, who he was stolen from as a baby, suggests that there is something important about his lineage, and about his status as a son. Particularly, as a son who is separated from his mother. This is a common theme that runs throughout the *Mabinogi*, which has led to suggestions that in fact it is Mabon who is being spoken of throughout, under different names and guises. It has been suggested, and generally accepted, that the name *Mabinogi* itself relates to Mabon, as 'mab' means boy or son in Old Welsh, although etymological origins of the rest of the word have proved difficult to trace. I introduced this idea in *Modron*, but let's look at this in a little more depth, as it relates to Mabon himself rather than his illustrious mother.

We are not told in the stories who stole Mabon when he was a baby, who imprisoned him in the fortress at Gloucester, or why, which suggests this refers to an older myth, which was already known to the listeners. Other sons in the *Mabinogi* are also taken from their parents; Pryderi is stolen from his mother the queen, Rhiannon, when he too is a few days old, only to be returned as a youth and become king. Branwen's infant son Gwern is actually killed, tossed into a fiery cauldron by his jealous uncle, and Lleu Llaw Gyffes is rejected and cursed by his mother Arianrhod, and overcomes the taboos she lays upon him with the help of his uncle, the magician Gwydion.

It is the story of Pryderi that has the most similarity to the story of Mabon, leading some scholars to equate the two. William J Gruffyd suggests that at the root of both tales lies a seasonal myth, similar to that of Demeter and her lost daughter Persephone. This reading is one of the reasons that Mabon has come to be seen as a Celtic sun god, born at Yule and dying at the harvest, giving his name to the Autumn Equinox for many neopagans. This is, however, a modern interpretation, and his name was only given to the festival in the 1970's, as we will discuss later.

Later scholars, such as Caitlin Matthews, see Mabon as part of a threefold archetypal 'sacred masculine', that is revealed through the tales of the *Mabinogi*. Matthews also applies this framework to the Arthurian tradition, thus equating Arthur himself with Mabon. In this telling, the masculine deity is first the Mabon, the Divine Youth, who after his return from imprisonment proves himself to be a great king or hero, a Pendragon, before finally becoming a Pen Annwfn, or Lord of the Underworld. He is then reborn again as the Mabon, in an ever turning cycle of the seasons, life and death, and human psychology. In Matthew's telling, this is the central theme of all four branches of the *Mabinogi* and can be seen playing out in the Arthurian and Grail myths, too.

While many mythicists find her theory compelling, and see the presence of these archetypes in the Brythonic myths, other scholars point out that such an archetypal reading is being superimposed on the text, giving it a meaning that it was most likely never intended to have. Many neopagans working within a Celtic tradition today seek to read such texts as they are, seeking to know what our ancestors were trying to achieve in their telling. By doing so we can see the figures represented within them in the way that they were being presented to the reader (or originally, the listener).

Searching for evidence that a mythical or literary character was inspired by an earlier deity is one thing; reading that mythical character entirely through the lens of modern archetypal theory is another.

In my view, both approaches have something to offer, but I take the criticisms of divorcing a text from its original meaning seriously. Working with archetypes and seeing them in mythology is a big part of many spiritual practices – and even organized religions, though they may use different terms – and gives the tales a life they may not otherwise have. A purely academic approach can be and has been criticized as deconstructing a text and leaving it as a dead thing, rather than a living myth that has something to offer each new generation that hears it. The tales in the *Mabinogi* were mostly intended to be told orally, and would have changed subtly with each telling, either with the passage of time or the chosen emphasis of the storyteller playing to a specific audience. And while archetypal psychology is a modern discipline, the fact that mythology contains timeless truths and shared motifs across time and culture is part of what makes it mythology. To read any text through a spiritual lens is to read it looking for deeper meaning, for symbols and metaphors that speak to us on a deeper level than historical facts ever can. Stories take on a meaning beyond the teller; the inspiration of the Celtic bardic *awen* comes through.

Nevertheless, texts such as the *Mabinogi* are not timeless but belong to a specific time and a specific culture, and are rooted in a history they cannot simply be lifted root and branch out of. The *Mabinogi* is a medieval Welsh text, written down in a time when Christianity had taken hold in Britain and much of the history of the Brythonic Celts had become lost to us. It should also be remembered that Wales was colonized by the English, and the Welsh language brutally suppressed in many areas. The tales deserve to be handled with respect by both scholars and spiritual seekers.

Perhaps one approach to these tales and the practices they inspire, and one that I shall try to take, is to make it clear whether we are speaking historically or archetypally/theologically, and to make it clear when a practice or belief comes from one's own personal experiences rather than historical example or a deity's original worship; as well as when an interpretation is being speculated rather than evidenced.

As a relevant example, I do personally relate to the concept of Modron and Mabon being celebrated at Yule, and to the Mother giving birth to the Son as allegorical to the birth of light in the darkness. Yet I am aware that this is mostly a modern interpretation and practice, heavily influenced by Christian and Classical mythology, and not one based in the texts or, as far as we know, the beliefs of the ancient Celts themselves. Yule itself is Germanic, not Celtic, in origin.

Of course, there is also middle ground. The study of ancient culture and myth must necessarily involve some educated speculation, because stories change and archaeological evidence can be interpreted in a variety of ways.

So, while celebrating Mabon at Yule or the Autumn Equinox is thoroughly modern, it is at least possible, given that marking the seasons was important to the Celts and indeed across the Indo-

European world, and that there was much syncretism between Celtic and Roman culture, that Gruffydd is not too far off the mark when suggesting that a seasonal myth may lie behind the figures of Modron and Mabon. We simply, as yet, do not know.

Mabon, Son of Mellt

Another allegory that Gruffydd saw in the *Mabinogi* was that of the Divine Family, which was influential among early neopagans. The Divine Father for Mabon, and consort for Modron, that Gruffydd proposes is Gwgon Gwron, who Gruffydd equates with the British Vironos, or 'Divine Man'. The issue with this is that nowhere is Mabon or Modron directly equated with this Gwgon Gwron, who is listed in the Welsh *Triads* as being the son of Peredur. As the Arthurian hero Peredur is sometimes equated with Pryderi, who is in turn equated with Mabon (Telyndru, 2023) this seems muddled.

Gwgon Gwron is, however, listed as the husband of St Madryn, often believed to be a Christianised version of Modron, so these figures do all seem to be entwined in some way that is yet to be unraveled, but to slot them neatly into a nuclear family requires a great deal of conjecture.

So, who is Mabon's father? It is notable that Mabon is one of the only figures in the *Mabinogi* to be introduced with his maternal rather than paternal heritage (Gwydion, son of Don being another) which may link him back to an earlier time when the Brythonic Celts, or certain tribes at least, traced their descent through the mother rather than the father. This is in keeping with the idea that Mabon's part of the tale is older than the rest, as this matrilineal custom is believed to have been part of the Neolithic cultures that Indo-European groups – which included the Celts – integrated with. The Indo-Europeans themselves are believed to have had mostly patriarchal customs.

But there may be a hint of Mabon's father in *Culhwch and Olwen*. After Mabon, son of Modron is freed, Arthur goes to seek the hounds that are needed, including Drudwyn, with a character called Mabon son of Mellt. Of course, this could be a separate character, but he is not otherwise mentioned, and once Drudwyn has been captured Mabon son of Mellt is described as handling him; something only Mabon son of Modron is able to do. This would indicate that they are the same person. Mellt has been translated as 'lightning,' which leads to speculation that Mabon was originally the son of a Mother Goddess (Modron meaning Great or Divine Mother) and a god of lightning. Again, if any such myth existed it is currently lost to us.

Mabon son of Mellt is again mentioned in the poem *Pa gur yv y Porthaur?* (Who is the Gatekeeper?) from the *Black Book Of Carmarthen*, or MS Peniarth 1, a fragmentary poem which shows Arthur boasting of the exploits of his men to a porter, while trying to gain entrance to a castle. He introduces Mabon, son of Modron, as 'a servant of Uther Pendragon' and says nothing of his prowess, while a few lines later he states that 'Mabon, son of Mellt spotted the grass with blood.' Given that this Mabon son of Mellt is never mentioned elsewhere or alone, and the clue mentioned above concerning his handling of Drudwyn, it seems reasonable to assume that this is another name for Mabon son of Modron. Which leaves the mysterious 'Mellt' as his father; or perhaps 'son of lightning' is a title, hinting at supernatural origins, an earlier deity status, or a miraculous birth from the Mother Goddess. Either way, Mabon's inclusion in this poem suggests that he also functions as a warrior, or as one of Arthur's knights. This is confirmed in another Mabinogi tale, *The Dream of Rhonabwy*, where Mabon son of Modron is listed as one of Arthur's 'counselors' at the Battle of Badon.

A poem attributed to Taliesin, *Englynion y Beddau* (Stanzas of the Graves) consists of a long verse listing the graves of the legendary Brythonic heroes. About Mabon it says 'The grave on the upland of Nantlle; No-one knows his remarkable characteristics, Mabon ap Modron the swift.' Nantlle Valley is in Gwynedd, North Wales and is a place of natural beauty, recognised for its connection to both Mabon and Modron and other tales in the *Mabinogi*. Seekers still visit the potential site of Mabon's grave, and there has been some speculation in New Age communities about a ley line running through the area.

Mabon and Owain

Mabon (son of Modron) is mentioned in a few other medieval texts, including the *Triads*. Triad 52 lists him as one of three 'Exalted Prisoners' along with Llyr and Gweir son of Geirionydd (more on this in Chapter 5.)

There is also a Mabon, with no mention of parentage, in *The Book of Taliesin*, a collection of medieval poetry attributed to the legendary bard Taliesin, who had the pseudo historical king Urien of Rheged as a patron. Many of Taliesin's poems draw on the same story themes and characters found in the *Mabinogi*, although Mabon here is not a divine son or an exalted prisoner but a warrior. He is mentioned briefly in *In the King of Heaven's Name, They Remember* as a fierce leader who fought against Gwallag, a sixth century contemporary of Urien, and left no survivors on the battlefield, but no more information is given.

In their translation notes, Lewis and Williams (2019) identify this Mabon as a tribal leader possibly named after the legendary Mabon, but not himself in any way supernatural. However, another poem, *News Has Reached Me from Calchfynydd*, focuses on a battle between warriors of the North and features Owain, Urien's son, and Mabon, a Northern leader who is presumably the same Mabon who fought against Gwallag. There are hints here that this Mabon is more than a historical, or even pseudo-historical, figure; he is 'a powerful man of fire,' and 'a white heat in the land,' which resonates with Mabon son of Modron being both 'swift' and a 'son of lightning.' Most telling is that Taliesin's Mabon rides a 'fierce white horse' just like Mabon in *Culhwch and Olwen*, and a white horse, as with any white

9

animal, is often a symbol that the person or animal is from the Otherworld, called in Welsh Annwn or Annwfn. It is also significant, as we shall see in the next chapter, that he is from the North.

But something even more interesting may be going on in this poem. Owain himself is frequently associated with Mabon, because his mother in the *Triads* is none other than Modron, the Great Mother herself, who becomes a consort to Urien of Rheged. This would make Mabon and Owain brothers. We may be looking at a mythical family feud here, a jostling of myths, or even the light and dark aspects of the same mythical persona. As with many of these texts, it is often difficult to tell what should be read mythically, historically or even satirically.

It also depends on the translation, and perhaps Lewis and Williams are being too conservative. Where they write 'Mabon from far away,' Prof. John Koch, whose work *The Celtic Heroic Age* is considered exemplary, translates this as 'Mabon from the other-realm.' Where they have simply 'From Mabon,' he has 'In the realm of Mabon.' Reading Koch's translation, one can immediately associate this Mabon with the imprisoned youth from the *Mabinogi*, although his persona has become substantially fiercer.

It is not immediately clear in this poem whether Mabon is for or against Owain, or whether the title 'Mabon' is being used to praise Owain himself. If this is true, then it is likely that the Mabon who fights Gwallag actually refers to Owain. The historical Taliesin was Urien's bard and therefore required to sing legendary songs of him and his progeny, so giving Owain a mythic title that meant 'Great Son' would have been wholly appropriate. The poems of Taliesin (or those writing in his name, as they span centuries) often refer to legendary characters known to us from the *Mabinogi* and *Triads,* and the later, more mystical poems are full of rich metaphor and reference to mythic themes. In another poem, *Primary Chief Bard*, 'Mabon' is twice used to refer to Christ himself, as the 'merciful Mabon,' and the 'Maiden's Mabon.' So we have some evidence that the bards and storytellers indeed used the word 'Mabon' to refer to various 'divine sons,' and not just the character of Mabon as we find him in *Culhwch and Olwen*. Bromwich (2006) suggests that Taliesin uses Mabon as a pseudonym for Owain, and Telyndru (2023) suggests that a potential linguistic root for *Owain* is *eoghunn*, which means 'youth.'

It could be possible then, although this is speculative, that the Mabon in *Culhwch and Olwen* is in fact Owain himself, especially given their shared motherhood, although it should be noted that there is no separate tale of Owain being snatched from Modron while a baby and imprisoned. Neither is Owain ever listed in the *Triads* as a prisoner – although Mabon is. In *Ghosts of the Forest*, an exploration of the landscape and myths of the Brythonic North, William A. Young (2022) traces Owain's lineage and shows that he is a divine son on both sides, as Urien was sometimes described as also being of supernatural parentage. Young explicitly equates Owain with Mabon. He also believes that the Arthurian romance *The Lady of the Well*, another tale included in the *Mabinogi*, offers hints that allow us to construct a fuller version of Mabon's mythos.

The Lady of the Well features Owain as its hero and is dated to the 13th century, and has much in common with the Arthurian tales of Chrétien de Troyes, leading some scholars to suggest that it is derived from de Troyes, while others postulate that they both spring from an older, shared root, most likely the work of Geoffrey of Monmouth, author of the *Vita Merlini*. In the tale, Owain is, as he appears in many other Arthurian tales, a champion in Arthur's court and one of his famed knights. Owain hears of the tale of a magical castle tended by beautiful maidens – which by description the reader can recognise is situated in an Otherworldly realm – and a mysterious well-guarded by an unbeatable Black Knight who has dominion over the wild animals. He finds the castle and stays the night there, tended to by the maidens, and then finds the well and defeats the Black Knight. Following this he is trapped inside another great, shining castle, until one of the aforementioned maidens, known as Luned, comes to him. He hears wailing overnight, and it transpires it is coming from a beautiful woman, the Lady of the Well, and that the Black Knight Owain killed was her husband. Despite this, she is persuaded to marry Owain, and he spends three years in the role of the Black Knight, defending the well, until Arthur requests that he visit the court. Owain goes back to Arthur, but stays for three years instead of three months, until the lady sends one of her women to reprimand him. For reasons not explained, instead of going back to the well and the lady, Owain wanders in the wilderness until he becomes little more than a beast, covered in hair and living with the wild animals. He is rescued by a widowed countess who heals him with a magical ointment. When a local earl lays siege to the countess, Owain rides out to meet him and gets the better of him. After this, Owain continues on his travels. He makes friends with a lion who he rescues from a serpent; the lion turns out to be none other than a shapeshifted Luned, who from then on becomes a helper to Owain, almost a totem animal. Luned helps him to defeat another evil knight and the 'Black Oppressor,' who mends his ways and opens a hostel for travelers. Finally, Owain returns to Arthur to become captain of his retinue, before returning to his own people, which includes an army of ravens. Owain and his army of ravens are also featured in *The Dream of Rhonabwy*.

The Lady of the Well is a very different story from the imprisonment and release of Mabon, and although they share motifs of shapeshifted wild animals and imprisonment in castles, there is nothing that immediately suggests any connection to Mabon other than Owain himself. The maidens of the castles and the lady who guards the well are common Grail themes which, as I discuss in more detail in *Modron*, carry echoes of Sovereignty myths, but here the goddess figure is a spouse, not a mother. While I remain unconvinced of Young's thesis, it is an interesting one and offers another potential lens through which to see the figure of Mabon. For it is certainly possible that the later legends attached to the pseudo historical figure of Owain ap Urien were derived from Mabon, his supernatural brother, and the mythos of his goddess mother.

Before we leave the *Mabinogi*, we should also, in light of the discussion of Owain, take a look at the story of *Peredur*, another of the three Arthurian romances contained within it. In this tale, Peredur is a youth who has various adventures on his quest to join Arthur's court as a knight. Owain features in the tale, in something of a mentor role to the clearly younger Peredur, and many of the adventures that Peredur has, involving castles, maidens and battling fierce knights, are reminiscent of Owain's in *The Lady of the Well*. An encounter with the Fisher King makes the story also very like that of de Troyes *Perceval*, and again it has been suggested that it either borrows from de Troyes or they are both using the same source.

There is much that can be said about all of these tales and their shared mythical themes, but what is significant for our purposes is the mention of Caerloyw ('Shining Fortress') as the home to the nine witches that Peredur has to battle. Caerloyw is the place where Mabon was imprisoned. Chapter 5 will look into Mabon's imprisonment in more detail, but we should note here that, as Telyndru states, Peredur is sometimes considered a later reflex of Pryderi, who has been regularly associated with Mabon. It seems likely that the *Mabinogi* indeed refers to tales of Mabon, not as a single figure but as many, with shared themes. It may also be 'stories of sons,' written perhaps for the sons of the medieval Welsh gentry. It is tempting to try to reconstruct a potential single myth for Mabon, or even the older Maponus, which then became fragmented into the various different stories, and we will return to this idea later.

Moving on from the medieval texts, we also find mention of Mabon in the Christian saints of Wales and Cornwall; clustered around the same areas where St Madryn, the potentially Christianised version of Modron, is also found. There is a Saint Mabon's Church in the parish of Llanfabon (the name of the parish derives from Mabon) near Pontypridd, and a church and village called St Mabyn in Bodmin, Cornwall. This St Mabyn is depicted as female, although in his *Lives of the Saints* Baring-Gould states that St Mabyn was actually male. Another Welsh St Mabon is known as St Mabon the Confessor, brother of St Llewellyn. There is very little known about these saints, which may be a clue that they were not historical figures at all, but rather Christianised Celtic deities or spirits.

Chapter 2

Maponus, Apollo and the *Locus Maponi*

In first century Britain and Gaul, the gods were rarely represented in image and nothing was written down; theirs was an oral culture. This changed with the growth of the Roman Empire, when the Romans built altars to both their own and local indigenous gods, often marrying the two in acts of syncretism that, while no doubt influencing and possibly changing indigenous worship, also helped to preserve evidence of it.

The Roman army, often made up of soldiers from the very areas the Romans had colonized, was particularly responsible for the spread of various deities, including those of the Celtic Britons and Gauls. Soldiers would also adopt the worship of local gods in the hope of gaining their protection while they were far from home. Indigenous beliefs influenced Roman culture too; as Miranda Aldhouse-Green (2023) states in *Sacred Britannia*, it was far from a one-way street.

The military north along Hadrian's Wall has proved a particularly fertile area for the discovery of various inscriptions and altars devoted to Celtic-Romano gods. A common god invoked in this area was Maponus, which means 'great son' or 'divine youth' and he is cognate with the later Mabon, just as the Celtic mother goddess Matrona (Great Mother) is cognate with Modron. The prefix *mapo*, meaning 'youth' or 'son' is Gaulish, and in the Brythonic tongues it becomes *mab*, and *macc* in the Old Irish, as in the Irish god of youth, Aengus mac Og.

Mabon and Modron, as Maponus and Matrona (who also seems to have had a triple aspect as the three mothers, the Matres or Matronae) were worshiped across Gaul and into Britain. As Matrona originated as the goddess of the river Marne, it is likely that her worship originated in Gaul and was spread northwards. However, although it seems undoubted that they are the same figures, Maponus is never described as the son of Matrona in the way that Mabon is so frequently associated with his goddess mother. It may be that they became intertwined later on and were not originally twinned, despite their names.

This twinning perhaps occurred because Maponus was frequently associated in Britain with the Roman god Apollo, also a youthful god of light and hunting, as well as healing and music. Aldhouse-Green points out that the pairing of a sun god or god of light with a goddess of the land was common among the Celts in this period, and while Matrona was a river goddess, she was also associated with the fertility of the land and with the figure of the goddess of Sovereignty, something I discuss in *Modron; Meeting the Celtic Mother Goddess*. In this vein, in Classical mythology storm or sky gods are often the father of sun gods…as Zeus with his lightning bolts is the father of Apollo. Is it too much of a stretch to wonder whether this is where 'Mabon, son of Mellt,' originated?

There is some evidence to suggest that Maponus was seen as the son of Matrona earlier than his twinning with Apollo, however. Bourbonne-les-Bain, a thermal spring near the source of the River Marne, and close to a temple dedicated to Matrona, was also the site of a funerary inscription mentioning the name Maponus. It also may have been the Gaulish Parisi tribe, whose territory was near the Marne, who brought the worship of Maponus to Britain (or vice versa). Carey and Koch suggest so, although other scholars believe the British Parisi spread to Gaul rather than the other way around, or that Maponus was the tribal god of the Arverni rather than Parisi. The history here is by no means settled. But whoever brought Maponus to or from Britain, once here the Romans twinned him decisively with their own Divine Youth figure, Apollo.

Mabon and Apollo

Two northern English altars, found along the east of Hadrian's Wall, are dedicated to Apollo Maponi and another to Mapono Apollini. On one, he is shown with a lyre. Another relief showing him with a lyre has been found near Blackpool. Lyres – or harps – were associated, as the first century Roman historian Diodorus tells us, with the Celtic bards. A fifth inscription occurs along Hadrian's Wall, naming him here purely as 'the holy god' Deo Mapono, with no Apollo attached. The area around Hadrian's Wall has also yielded numerous dedications to the Matronae, although not to Matrona as a single figure. A goddess figure has been found with no inscription, which looks very like statues of Matrona, but it should be remembered that many of the features of Matrona's statues in Gaul were similar to those of other mother goddesses.

We don't know how many of Maponus' associations were shared with Apollo, leading to their linkage, and which were later added to his veneration due to his having been twinned with Apollo. There is little in Mabon's later story or Maponus' iconography to suggest an association with light, other than the fact that Caerloyw means 'Shining Fortress,' and so the idea of him as a sun god may have originally come from his association with Apollo. The Roman deities were not necessarily a perfect fit for the Celtic deities they were matched to; it was enough that their prominent associations were the same. With this in mind it's worth taking a look at certain aspects of Apollo, who himself is a complex and potentially very old deity.

Like the sons of the *Mabinogi* he was endangered as a baby, although in Apollo's myth his pregnant mother Leto saves him from Hera's wrath by shapeshifting into a wolf and giving birth to him on a floating island with the help of Poseidon. In some versions, Poseidon brings the island underwater so that the laboring Leto can be hidden from Hera. The labor lasts nine days and nine nights and results in Apollo and his twin sister Artemis, also a goddess of hunting and hounds.

Apollo is described in the Ancient Greek texts as a beautiful youth, golden like the sun and swift of foot, and often seen either with a bow and arrow or his famous lyre. He is also associated with healing and prophecy, and various animals including eagles and dolphins. He also has his darker side; he was associated with cursing as well as healing, and one of his epithets calls him a bringer of plague. Many of his myths show him to be capricious and cruel. As we have no remaining myths of Maponus, and scant information on Mabon, we cannot know how many of these attributes were originally shared, or which attributes made the Romans twin Maponus with Apollo. It is important to remember that there is likely to be as much Classical influence on the stories of the *Mabinogi* as there is Christian.

Healing and Harpers

The association with healing is not one that we find in Mabon's story either, but it is correlated with Maponus, due to an inscription to him being found at the healing spring at Source des Roches at Chamalieres in France. Just as Matrona originated as a river goddess, Maponus may have his origins as the local deity of the spring, making him a water god also.

The amount of votive offerings found at the site indicate that it was an incredibly important place to the local Celts as a place to petition the gods for healing, and a tablet has been found there, with an inscription to Maponus which Carey and Koch translate as beseeching him to 'quicken us by the magic of the underworld spirits.' In the ancient world, sickness and disease was often viewed as being caused by malicious spirits, just as benevolent spirits had the power to heal, and it seems here that Maponus is being called on to use his assumed authority over those spirits. This is a traditionally shamanic function, a mediation between this world and the Otherworld to bring about healing, and we will look at shamanic elements in Mabon's story in the next chapter.

Dogs were also frequently associated with healing along with hunting, and we have seen that Mabon was said to be the only hunter who could handle the hound Drudwyn. Coming back to the north of what is now England, and stretching into the south of Scotland, we find an area which shows evidence of having been the site of a cult of Maponus worship. The *Ravenna Cosmography*, written in 700 CE, lists an area in the North known as *locus Maponi*, or 'the place of Maponus' and there are place names in the area that may refer to him, such as Lochmaben in southern Scotland and Clachmabenstane, a standing stone in Gretna Green. In what may be an echo of folk memory, there is a ballad known as the 'Harper of Lochmaben' which dates from Tudor times, and was included in a collection by Francis Child in the nineteenth century. One version of it has the first verses as

HARD ye tell of the silly blind harper?
Long he lived in Lochmaben town;
He's away to fair Carlisle,
To steal King Henry's Wanton Brown

He has mounted his auld gray mare,
And ridden oer both hills and mire,
Till he came to fair Carlisle town,
And askd for stabling to his mare

If there is a folk memory of Maponus/Mabon here then it is much changed from its original source, but it is interesting that Lochmaben, believed to be named for Mabon, is associated with a harper on a gray mare (white horses were also called grays) given Maponus' association with the harp or lyre and Mabon's white horse.

The Place of Mabon

The poem about Owain and Mabon in *The Book of Taliesin*, which we looked at in the last chapter, may be referring to this area when it speaks of Mabon having come from his own country, somewhere to the north. Given that this area is close to where the kingdom of Urien and Owain is believed to have been, this lends some weight to Young's idea that Owain was seen as a reflex of Mabon, or at least that local memories of the cult of Maponus made their way into the tales of Urien and Owain.

Apollo too was often associated with the north in his guise as the 'Hyperborean Apollo.' Hyperborea was a mystical land at the north of the world, according to the Classical Greeks, and (in what is likely to be a seasonal myth about the sun, potentially centered around the Winter Solstice and the darkest period of the year) for a month every year Apollo went there. While he was gone, his oracular temple of Delphi shut down and could not function. Herodotus in his *Histories* links Hyperborea to Delos, the floating island of Apollo's birth, stating that the people of Delos worshiped the Hyperboreans. In the 4th century BC Diodorus linked Britain itself with Hyperborea, the lands of the north.

Almost halfway between Lochmaben and Clachmabenstane an archaeological find in the 1960's revealed a stone slab with a crude drawing of a dog and the inscription 'a basket for Maponus.'

Cunomaglos and Nodens

This association with both dogs and Apollo has led researchers, such as Ralph Hausller (2018) to speculate that Maponus was also connected to the deity known in Wiltshire as Cunomaglos, or 'houndlord,' who was also linked with Apollo. Haussler believes Cunomaglos and Maponus were seen as powerful deities and perhaps as different aspects of one deity.

Apollo Cunomaglos had a temple at Nettleton Shrub in Wiltshire which was situated on the Fosse Way, making it likely to have been visited often by travelers, as Aldhouse-Green suggests. She believes the obvious importance of the temple, which seems to have been a place of pilgrimage – perhaps a place where pilgrims could stay overnight in a lodge in the hope of receiving dreams from the gods – indicates that Cunomaglos was an important deity well before the arrival of the Romans. The temple may have been popular as a site of healing, and this reinforces a deeper symbolism of the houndlord as a healer, and dogs as animals associated with healing and the Otherworld, something also seen across the Classical world such as in the cult of Asklepios.

Another deity, although one twinned with Mars rather than Apollo, who shares the dogs, healing and hunting motifs and is found in Gloucester where Mabon was imprisoned, is Nodens. Although there is nothing to directly connect Mabon and Nodens, he was also a god of dreams, and had a temple at Lydney in Gloucester which may have been a dream sanctuary, just as Aldhouse-Green suggests Cunomaglos had at Nettleton Shrub. Nodens is also believed to be cognate with 'Nudd,' as in Gwyn ap Nudd, that other great mythical huntsman in *Culhwch and Olwen.* This is not to suggest that Mabon is Nodens is Cunomaglos or vice versa, but it is intriguing that these gods, with similar associations, symbols and possibly practices are found in close proximity. For those neopagans who see the gods as being facets of a greater whole, these deities are perhaps personifying the same energies and principles. From a purely historical perspective, while this is conjecture on my part, the fact that Nodens and Mabon are both tied to Gloucester may indicate that at some point the myths and/or worship of Nodens and Maponus/Mabon became entwined, or perhaps that of Nodens and Cunomaglos, who may have been at some point associated with Maponus, or even been a specifically localized version of him.

What is most interesting to me about all of these gods, however, is that gods of hunting seem to be often also gods of healing, or dreams, or as the tablet found at Chamalieres suggests, of communicating with the spirits and the Under or Otherworld

There is a sense of something wild about a god of the hunt, and of something more ancient than the world of militarized Roman Britain. Let's look again at the story of the hunting of the Twrch Trwyth, and what this may tell us about the figure of Mabon.

Chapter 3

The Hunter and the Hound

Hunting myths are some of the oldest – if not *the* oldest – myths that we have, and have been associated with Paleolithic cave art. The original hunting myth is believed to have been born in what is now Northern Russia, before spreading over the rest of the world – particularly Eurasia and the Americas. It typically involved only one or a few hunters, and one animal, often a horned animal such as an elk or deer, although this varied across cultures, eventually becoming as diverse as bears, caribou or camels. The story was linked to the stars, in particular the constellations we know now as Orion and Ursa Major. (Berezkin, 2005)

Academics believe the original hunting myth could be older than twenty-five thousand years, and reflects the day to day lives of our ancient ancestors, for whom hunting was directly linked to survival. This was true too for the earliest Britons living on a land which was much colder than we are used to (for all our complaints about British weather!) and covered in pine forest. There was little in the way of edible plants, meaning that foraging was limited and hunting and fishing the main sources of food. Elk and reindeer were plentiful and therefore would have been a primary food source. The earliest religion in Britain would have likely been similar to what we know of Siberian shamanism, due to similar living conditions and a focus on hunting and animals. Archaeological finds at Star Carr in Yorkshire have included headdresses that are eleven thousand years old, made of animal skulls, mostly antlered deer skulls, which were likely used as the basis for ritual practices around the hunting of red deer, making them our earliest known shamanic artifacts. (Coneller, 2016) This seems to have been a widespread practice, with similar headdresses found across Europe.

'Deer dances' such as the Abbot Bromley Horn Dance may trace their origins back to the beliefs and practices of our Mesolithic ancestors, especially as similar dances are found in other cultures as far apart as Siberia and Native American tribes, giving weight to the theory of a widespread ancient hunting myth that inspired – or was drawn from – shamanic practices.

By 'shamanism,' I am referring to a religious or spiritual practice that involves communicating with the spirit world, such as ancestors, spirits of animals or nature spirits, via altered states of consciousness. Consciousness can be altered via trance or psychoactive substances. Although the word itself is specific, originating in Siberia, these types of practices are believed to be found across the world, with some forms believed to have originated in the Palaeolithic.

Shamanism is currently undergoing a revival in religious, pagan and New age circles, and a 2023 census in England and Wales showed that neo-shamanism is the fastest growing religion/spirituality, increasing more than tenfold in a decade. Unfortunately, this rise has come with a tendency towards cultural appropriation of indigenous spirituality, particularly of Native American and Aboriginal ritual. In an attempt to counter this, as well as connect with ancestral traditions, many Western neopagans look to Celtic and Norse traditions, or Western traditions such as the Eleusinian Mysteries. While we may not be able to perfectly recreate these (and probably wouldn't want to, given that our ancestors had very different world views and lifestyles) we can be inspired by and draw from what we learn about their practices and traditions. Hints of shamanic practice can be seen in our old tales, and many researchers see a shamanic spirit in the Celtic bardic tradition. Modern Druids often draw on this, with the British Druid Order in particular framing our Druidic past as shamanic in origin.

Hounds

Hunting myths remained popular even after we transitioned to agriculture and began to hunt less. Apollo himself, along with his twin sister the goddess Artemis, was a hunting deity. To this day we have folktales of Gwyn ap Nudd (who also joins Arthur and Mabon to hunt the Twrch Trwyth) and the Wild Hunt, and his Otherworldly hounds streaming down Glastonbury Tor in pursuit of their prey. This hunting and hound deity, or spirit, seems to be widespread across cultures, taking on different facets both between and among them.

We don't know whether Maponus was a hunting deity before he became twinned with Apollo, but it's possible that it was this association which connected them, especially as Maponus seems to have been linked with hounds. The hunter and his hound have come down to us in Mabon's role in *Culhwch and Olwen.*

We also don't know enough about the deities of Celtic Britain and Gaul to say how they were connected to these earlier hunting myths. Was the Maponus of Northern Britain a local deity whose worship existed in some form before the arrival of the people we know as the Celts, his roots going back to our shamanic past, or did these elements become entwined with Maponus/Mabon later on? We have as yet little evidence to back up any speculation, but we do know that the mythical hunting motifs themselves are incredibly ancient and stretch back to our Paleolithic past.

Mabon is not just any hunter; like Gwyn ap Nudd, he is from the Otherworld. We know this, not just from his epithet, but because he has been imprisoned for centuries, well beyond any normal lifespan, and also because both his horse and his hound are pure white (though his horse may have had a brown or dun mane) a common motif of an Otherworldly animal in Celtic myth. The boar they are hunting is also white, and later revealed in the story to have once been a human king.

He is also, like Cunomaglos, a houndlord. For only 'one man in the whole world' can handle the Otherworldly dog Drudwyn, and 'he is Mabon son of Modron.' This is potentially hinting at older stories of Mabon that have been lost, as we aren't told why Mabon is the only hunter skilled enough to handle Drudwyn. As far as we know, he has been imprisoned since he was three nights old, so where did he come by this seemingly legendary prowess? He may have something in common with Gwyn ap Nudd in that he is not just from the Otherworld but a king – or in Mabon's case, a prince – of it. In the *Triads* his mother Modron is listed as the daughter of Afallach, a king of Annwfn, the Otherworld, putting Mabon firmly in a royal lineage of Annwfn.

The entire story of the hunting of the Twrch Trwyth is reminiscent of the Wild Hunt motif, which is found in myth and folklore across Northern Europe.

The leader of the Wild Hunt is usually a mythological figure, the hunters are from the Otherworld, or are souls of the dead, and the hounds are ghostly – possibly white, like Drudwyn. In a more Christianised version, the lead hunter is the Devil, and demons are his host. (Lecouteux, 2011) To watch the Wild Hunt can drag the onlooker straight to hell. The hunting of the boar Twrch Trwyth in order to acquire the comb, razor and shears for Ysbaddaden is tame by comparison to these diabolic versions, which were often written down by clergy.

The inclusion of hounds in hunting myths is nearly as old as the myths themselves, reflecting the twelve thousand years that humans and dogs have been teaming up. Dogs and humans were companions long before we were riding horses, farming cows or keeping chickens. It's perhaps not surprising then that dogs turn up as Otherworldly spirits in so many mythologies, including the Celtic. The Cwn Annwn, the hounds of the Otherworld who were white with red ears, were also part of the Wild Hunt, and took on the role of running wrongdoers into the ground. The hunting dog is often seen as being represented in the stars as Canis Major, just as the hunter is represented as Orion. In local Welsh folklore, Orion is Mabon, and Canis Major is Drudwyn. The hunter and his hound are inseparable.

Horses

Mabon's horse, too, is special. He has to have a specific horse, Gwynn Mygdwn, who belongs to a warrior called Gweddw. Gwynn Mygdwn means either 'White Dun Mane' or 'White Hacked Mane.' Rachel Bromwich associates the horse with *Triad 46a* which mentions 'Arched Mane, Horse of Gweddw' as one of the 'Three Bestowed Horses of Britain.'

Horses were prominent in the mythology of Britain and Ireland, and the horse goddess Epona was worshiped across Roman Gaul, including by the Romans themselves. In Britain, a small bronze statue of her has been found, seated between two horses. Rhiannon's association with horses has led to speculation that the roots of Rhiannon's myth go back to the worship of Epona, although some scholars are skeptical of this. In Irish legend, Macha was forced to take part in a horse race while pregnant, resulting in her cursing the men of Ulster. Horses are thus associated with justice, fertility and Sovereignty, and white horses in particular with the Otherworld. The Celtic Dobunni tribe, whose lands stretched from Gloucester to Warwickshire, are believed to have had the horse as their totem, due to the prominence of horse images on their coins. The Dobunni moved into South Wales after being defeated by the Saxons, and it has been suggested that they brought their tales of the horse goddess with them, which may later be echoed in the tales of Rhiannon and Pryderi, who is associated with the foal.

This reverence for horses wasn't limited to the tribes that we know today as the 'Celts;' the White Horse of Uffington, a chalk outline of a horse carved into a hillside in Oxfordshire, may date back as far as 1380 BC. The white horse as possessing spiritual or Otherworldly significance is a motif that seems to have been shared across the Indo-European world. The Norse god Odin rode a supernatural eight-legged horse, the winged Pegasus was white, and Herodotus in his *Histories* reported that in the Persian culture of Xerxes, white horses were considered sacred, and could also be used as payment in exchange for land, which recalls the association with Sovereignty. In Christian myth, one of the Four Horsemen of the Apocalypse rides a white horse, and in Hinduism a white horse also appears in apocalyptic tales.

This widespread motif of the sacred white horse points at a Proto-Indo-European (PIE) root, as Kaliff and Oestigaard (2020) suggest. Sadly, it seems that the original rites relating to the sacred horse involved the sacrificing of it, and similar rituals involving horse sacrifice, Kaliff and Oestigaard's paper shows, were widespread from the Russian Steppes to Scandinavia to Western Europe, and may have been originally related to Bronze Age cosmogony and a belief in the need for sacrifice to maintain the cosmos.

Later, the horse sacrifice is associated with kingship and the fertility of the land, and the Indian Vedic *ashwamedha* ritual involved the prospective king letting a stallion roam free. Wherever the stallion roamed in a year was under the king's rule. The stallion was then sacrificed. A similar ritual believed to be practiced by Irish kings as recently as the twelfth century was described by Gerald of Wales. In the Irish rite it was not a stallion but a white mare, and the king allegedly mates with the mare before it is sacrificed, after which the king bathes in a broth made of its blood. Although Gerald's account of Irish customs is generally believed to be fantastical, the similarity of the ritual with others across the Indo-European world suggest there may have been some truth in the tale. As bizarre (and brutal) as these horse sacrifices sound to our ears today, the linking of the horse with the Sovereignty of the land is clearly illustrated.

In the *Mabinogi*, although Rhiannon on her white horse is considered a Sovereignty figure as she bestows the land of Dyfed upon Pwyll, white horses are also clearly linked with deities or spirits of the hunt. The Wild Hunt motif, particularly in its diabolic versions, is reminiscent of the earlier apocalyptic stories in which an Otherworldly figure or deity also rides a white horse. This would suggest that horses, and particularly white ones, were associated not just with fertility and kingship of the land but also with both death and the Otherworld.

Boars and Pigs

As well as hounds and horses, animals of all kinds are prominent in Celtic myth. The story of the rescue of Mabon is full of some very special animals, which we will look at in more detail in the next chapter. One more animal to consider in the context of Mabon the huntsman is the boar – the Twrch Trwyth himself.

Boars and pigs are prominent in Celtic myth, and there seems to be a particular status attached to them, no doubt on a partly practical level due to the fact that if you had a pig, you had a feast. Pork was prime feasting meat, and a pig or boar could feed a family for weeks. There are boars on the Gundestrup cauldron, along with the stag god Cernunnos, and in Celtic Gaul there were the boar god Euffigneix and the pig god Moccus, who seems to have had a significant cult associated with him. In Irish myth, the god Lugh had a magic pig skin that could cure any ailment. In the *Mabinogi*, a white sow leads Gwydion to the enchanted Lleu and the King of the Otherworld, Arawn, gives Pryderi a herd of pigs. Pryderi also later chases a white boar, another glaring similarity to Mabon, although Pryderi is imprisoned afterwards. The enchantress Ceridwen, mythical mother of the bard Taliesin and keeper of the cauldron of *awen*, the divine inspiration, is sometimes associated with pigs. Merlin runs wild with a boar in the Caledonian forest. In the tale of *Culhwch and Olwen*, Culhwch himself is born in a pigsty. Pigs have been demonized in some religions, but to the Celts they were honored animals and their meat was a prize.

Wild boars were once native to Britain and along with deer would have been a widely hunted animal. Sadly, they were hunted to extinction in the thirteenth century, not long after the tales in the *Mabinogi* were written down. Boars were ferocious and dangerous to hunt, but the reward was considered worth it. The Twrch Trwyth was the most ferocious of all; famously irate and with poisonous bristles, it is notable that it took an entire band of huntsmen that included the legendary Arthur, Gwyn ap Nudd and Mabon, and a variety of Otherworldly animals, to eventually bring him down. The boar lays waste to a fifth of Ireland in the process with his rampaging.

We first meet him in the ninth century *Historia Brittonum*, where he is listed alongside Arthur's dog Cafall. The boar has been transformed from a prince or king (his name may mean 'king's boar') due to his unspecified sins; this may be a Christian gloss of a much older story, as like much of *Culhwch and Olwen* there are references within this story that listeners may have been expected to already understand. Transformations from human to animal, sometimes as part of a curse, occur in other tales, such as Lleu Llaw Gyffes becoming an eagle. These are often read today as having shamanic undertones.

Shapeshifting

Perhaps the most famous of the shapeshifting myths in the Brythonic tradition is that of Taliesin and Cerridwen. Gwion Bach becomes a hare, a bird and even a grain of wheat in order to escape Cerridwen, who promptly becomes a hound, eagle and hen, eating him only to birth him nine months later as Taliesin. This undeniably shamanic sounding story lies at the heart of the Welsh bardic tradition, and many of Taliesin's poems (or those attributed to him) echo this tale. To use John Matthews' translation;

Since then I have fled in the shape of a crow,
since then I have fled as a speedy frog,
since then I have fled with rage in my chains,
– a roe-buck in a dense thicket.

I have fled in the shape of a raven of prophetic speech,
in the shape of satirizing fox,
in the shape of a sure swift,
in the shape of a squirrel vainly hiding.

I have fled in the shape of a red deer,
in the shape of iron in a fierce fire,
in the shape of a sword sowing death and disaster,
in the shape of a bull, relentlessly struggling.

I have fled in the shape of a bristly boar in a ravine,
in the shape of a grain of wheat.
I have been taken by the talons of a bird of prey
which increased until it took the size of a foal.

There are also echoes here of the Irish *Song of Amergin*

I am the sea blast
I am the tidal wave
I am the thunderous surf
I am the stag of the seven tines
I am the cliff hawk
I am the sunlit dewdrop
I am the fairest of flowers
I am the rampaging boar
I am the swift-swimming salmon
I am the placid lake
I am the summit of art
I am the vale echoing voices

I am the battle-hardened spearhead
I am the God who inflames desire
Who gives you fire
Who knows the secrets of the unhewn dolmen
Who announces the ages of the moon
Who knows where the sunset settles

These are beautiful, evocative lines that hint at a deeper, older and recognizably shamanic vein in the bardic tradition as well as in the Celtic myths and legends that fed it. The tale of the hunting of Twrch Trwyth, and of the freeing of Mabon, likely has its roots in this same vein, as we shall see more clearly in the next chapter when we look at how Mabon is found via the questioning of the Oldest Animals.

Celtic Shamanism

The word 'shaman' is itself Siberian, although 'shamanic' is now used to refer to a set of spiritual practices that we find in both old and new traditions. Shamanic practice, rooted in indigenous traditions from around the world, revolves around the shaman's ability to navigate between the physical realm and the spiritual dimensions. Central to shamanism is the concept of the shamanic journey, where the practitioner enters a trance-like state, often facilitated by rhythmic drumming, chanting, or plant medicines, in order to commune with spirits, seek guidance, and facilitate healing for individuals and communities.

These journeys often involve practitioners communicating with power animals, ancestral spirits, or nature deities, all of which may provide insight, protection, and assistance in the shaman's work. While tribal shamans tend to journey on behalf of the community or others seeking their help, modern-day shamanic practitioners may journey on their own behalf or in a group setting. If the idea of shamanic practice is new to you, it is very similar to many forms of guided journeying, creative visualization and even hypnotherapy. Practitioners vary on whether they see themselves as visiting the spirit world, the collective consciousness or exploring their own subconscious, but regardless, these encounters are not mere flights of fancy; they are potent experiences that can offer profound spiritual guidance and support.

While 'neo-shamanism' is considered a universal practice, greater awareness of cultural appropriation and racism towards indigenous minorities has led many neopagan practitioners to look to their own ethnic or community roots to seek ways to incorporate practices that could be termed 'shamanic.' The Celtic Bardic tradition, for example, is deeply intertwined with the rich tapestry of Celtic spirituality, storytelling, and artistic expression, and Celtic mythology as we have seen offers its own rich, 'shamanic' roots. This ancient and later medieval tradition, characterized by the role of the bard as a custodian of culture and wisdom, illuminates how guided journeying can be seen by some as a modern embodiment of the bard's mystical and transformative practices.

Within the Celtic tradition, bards were revered as poets, musicians, and storytellers who served as the keepers of the tribe's oral history, myths, and spiritual wisdom. They were the bridge between the mundane and the sacred, using their creative gifts to weave tales of heroism, love, and the mysteries of the cosmos. Bards were not just entertainers; they were often the spiritual guides and educators of their communities, offering insights into the deeper layers of existence. The tale of Mabon and the poetry of Taliesin and Amergin are examples of this strain of wisdom.

One of the most striking parallels between the Celtic Bardic tradition and guided journeying is the role of imagination and visualization. Bards were masters of the spoken word and the power of storytelling, using their words to transport their listeners to otherworldly realms and awaken the senses to the wonders of the unseen. Through vivid descriptions and poetic language, they could evoke landscapes, characters, and emotions, allowing their audience to partake in a shared journey of the mind and spirit

Guided journeying, as a modern practice, taps into this innate human capacity for imaginative storytelling. It invites individuals to embark on inner quests through the power of visualization. Just as bards used words to paint pictures in the minds of their audience, guided journeying employs guided meditations, drumming, or chanting to help participants vividly visualize sacred landscapes, encounters with spirit guides, and mystical experiences. In this way, it honors the Celtic Bardic tradition's reverence for the imaginative realm as a gateway to spiritual insight

Both the Celtic Bardic tradition and modern guided journeying often emphasize the importance of connecting with the land and the natural world. Celtic bards often drew inspiration from the landscapes, sacred sites, and natural elements of their homelands, infusing their tales with a profound sense of place and reverence for the earth.

Guided journeying or visualization can therefore be a potent and spiritually enriching practice which enables practitioners to explore the depths of their consciousness, connect with the energies of the natural world, and seek guidance from divine forces. Rooted in both indigenous ancient traditions and modern reinterpretations, guided visualization is a safe and simple way to begin exploring shamanic practice if this is something you are interested in, or a way to deepen your meditation or relaxation practice if you are not. At its core, journeying involves entering a state of altered consciousness, often induced through meditation or rhythmic drumming, allowing individuals to transcend the boundaries of ordinary perception. In this altered state, one can embark on an inner quest, traversing landscapes of the imagination, or connecting with the archetypal realms of the collective unconscious. Journeying can be a tool for introspection, healing, and personal growth, allowing individuals to confront inner conflicts, address unresolved emotions, and seek clarity on life's challenges.

What follows is a basic guided visualization that will allow you to begin exploring these practices in a gentle way, using deep relaxation to allow your mind to access the deeper layers of your imagination, using the image of Mabon as Lord of the Hunt. Psychologist Carl Jung believed in the importance of symbols and stories to our subconscious, and as explored above the symbol and the story of the hunt is deeply embedded in the human psyche.

To undertake the following guided journey, you can record the script and play it back to yourself, or ask someone you trust to read it out to you. Speak slowly and deeply and allow a pause after each sentence. Lie down in a quiet and safe space so that you won't be disturbed, and have a pen and paper close by in case you want to record any insights afterward. The process is gentle and relaxing, so don't fight it if you want to fall asleep; you may find your dreams are very interesting as a result! It is advisable not to try and drive or operate heavy machinery while listening or immediately afterwards, and individuals with any history of psychosis or severe trauma should consult their medical practitioner before trying guided journeying.

Journey to Meet the Huntsman

As you close your eyes and take a deep breath, you can begin with a gentle body scan, gradually becoming aware of each part of your being from head to toe. With each mindful breath, you release any tension or distraction, grounding yourself in the present moment and deeply relaxing your mind and body. As you exhale, release any tension from the crown of your head, around your eyes, your jaw, your neck, relaxing deeper and deeper. Breathe in a sense of relaxation and wellbeing, breathe out and let go, going deeper and deeper into relaxation. Release your shoulders, your chest, your arms, hands, fingers…breathe slowly in and out and relax your stomach and lower back, your hips and buttocks. Relax your legs, your feet, and each of your toes. As your breath gets longer and slower you relax deeper and deeper, drifting into that space between the worlds. Breathe in calm and wellbeing, breathe out, deep and long, and let go. Feel your body sinking deeper into relaxation, becoming heavy and quiet, your mind calm and still. Breathe in, relax, and breathe out, let go. Again, relax…let go. One more time, relax, and let go…

In your mind's eye now you can see yourself going down a set of dark wooden stairs, ten in all. As you go down I will count from ten to one, one step at a time, breathing more and more deeply as you go down. Ten…nine…going down now…eight, seven…deeper and deeper…six, five…more and more relaxed … … ..feeling safe and supported…four…three…nearly there now…two, one.

Now in your mind's eyes, you see yourself standing at the edge of a dense, mysterious forest at night. The air is cool, and the scent of earth and pine fills your senses. The moon, full and luminous, casts an ethereal glow upon the forest floor, illuminating a path that winds deeper into the heart of the woods. You follow the path instinctively.

With each step you take into the woods, the darkness envelops you, and the distant sounds of owls and night creatures serenade your journey. As you venture further into the forest, the trees seem to grow taller and older, their branches intertwining like gnarled fingers reaching out to the night sky. You are not scared as you sense the forest welcomes you, knows you, guiding you into its depths.

The path becomes a narrow trail, dappled with moonlight and shadow. You feel a sense of anticipation, a stirring in your soul, as if something significant awaits you atop the hill that you now find yourself walking up.

Climbing steadily, you soon reach the crest of the hill, and there, bathed in the moon's radiant glow, stands a majestic figure.

The Hunter God, tall and regal, with antlers adorning his head, sits atop a magnificent white horse. His eyes are like pools of ancient wisdom, they lock onto yours, and you feel a sense of recognition, a connection that transcends time and space. Without words, you understand that he is here to guide you on a quest, a sacred hunt. Only you know what it is that you are looking for.

He extends his hand, and you find yourself effortlessly mounting the back of his steed. The world takes on a different perspective as you become one with the horse, feeling the power and grace of the magnificent creature beneath you.

With a nod from the Hunter God, you set off at a swift and steady pace. Your senses sharpen as you become attuned to the forest around you. The wind rustles through the leaves, and the scent of the earth is rich and primal.

Moonbeams guide your way as you navigate through the labyrinthine forest, your heart beating in rhythm with the hoofbeats of the horse.

The Hunter God leads you deeper into the night, and it becomes clear that you are not hunting for physical prey but for a part of yourself that you have lost along the way. The forest, with its dark and mysterious depths, represents the uncharted territories of your inner world, and the moon serves as a beacon, illuminating the path to self-discovery.

As you ride alongside the Hunter God, you feel a transformation beginning to stir within you. The boundaries of your human form blur, and you undergo a metamorphosis as you leap down from the horse, stretching agile new limbs. You have become a hound, sleek and agile, with heightened senses and instincts. The world takes on new dimensions as you see, smell, and hear with the acute awareness of the canine.

Together with the Hunter God, you continue the hunt, not for an external quarry but for a part of yourself that you need to integrate. This is a hunt to retrieve the essence of your own self.

The forest seems to pulse with life, and you follow the scent of your own trail, tracking the echoes of your past experiences, choices, and emotions.

The Hunter God, a silent and steadfast presence by your side, offers guidance and support, reminding you of your own strength and resilience. The hunt takes you through valleys of doubt, thickets of fear, and clearings of forgotten joy. It's a journey of self-reflection, forgiveness, and acceptance. You confront your regrets and wounds, seeking to mend the fragments of your soul that have been scattered throughout the landscape of your life.

With each step and each moment of self-discovery, you feel a profound sense of wholeness and healing. As the hound, you are no longer separate from your own essence, and the sense of loss begins to fade away. The hunt becomes a celebration of self-reclamation, a reminder that every experience, every choice, has shaped the person you have become.

[Pause for a few moments and see where your mind takes you]

Eventually, as the moon reaches its zenith, you find yourself at a tranquil clearing bathed in moonlight. The Hunter God dismounts from his horse, and you, as the hound, sit beside him. There is a deep sense of fulfillment, knowing that you have found what you were seeking all along—a reconnection with your true self. In this sacred space, under the full moon's watchful gaze, you merge back into your human form.

The Hunter God smiles knowingly, his eyes filled with pride and approval. You have completed the hunt. With a sense of gratitude and newfound wisdom, you bid farewell to the Hunter God and his white steed.

You walk back down the hill and back through the forest. It is dawn now and the sky is light purple and the birds are beginning to sing. Feeling light and hopeful, you find the wooden stairs and begin to climb back up, returning to the present day. Becoming aware of your body again, of the room around you. Of your breath. Stretch your limbs, come back...And when you are ready you can open your eyes, and feel awake and refreshed.

Chapter 4

The Oldest Animals

As we saw in the last chapter, animals were important in the lives of the Celts, whether this involved hunting, farming, warfare or survival. Animal totems were used by many tribes – for the Dobunni, for example, it seems to have been the horse – and animals played important parts in various tales. We have looked at the hound, the horse and the boar, all associated with the tale of Mabon helping to hunt the Twrch Trwyth, and the antiquity of hunting myths themselves, but there are other animals in Mabon's tale who are significant, and also suggest an older origin to this part of the tale as well as imbuing it with a sense of the shamanic.

Arthur and his men ask five animals for Mabon's whereabouts. These are three birds; a blackbird, owl and eagle, then a stag and finally a salmon.

There is something strange about these animals (other than the fact that they can talk!) They are all ancient; unbelievably so, and each one that they encounter is older still. Yet none of them are older than Mabon's imprisonment, a fact which tells us, regardless of the actual given location of Gloucester, that Mabon's incarceration takes place in the Otherworld, out of ordinary time. Mabon's imprisonment is ancient, and yet he is forever a youth.

Legends of the oldest animals are found in many cultures, and one of the oldest versions is found in the Jataka, the mythical birth stories of the Buddha. In it, a partridge, a monkey and an elephant are the oldest animals, and it is revealed that the partridge – the most ancient of the three – is the Buddha himself. (Hull, 1932)

In Ireland a group of stories describes animals surviving the Biblical Flood in order to be able to relate the history of Ireland's mythical invasions from the Fomorians to the Milesians. In a 1981 paper by Michael Bath, he discusses a Hesiodic fragment which uses the Oldest Animals motif and the theory that it originated as a proverb, one which had hardened into a literary form by the time Hesiod was writing. Hesiod's oldest animals are crows, ravens, stags and phoenixes.

Birds, stags and salmon are common across the Classical and Celtic versions, as demonstrated in *Culhwch and Olwen*, as are dogs, horses and to add variety, oak trees. Which animal is the oldest varies across the tales, but as Bath points out, enough medieval and Renaissance authors, including Milton and Donne, alluded to the Oldest Animals to show that by this time knowledge of the motif was commonplace.

The ancient animals in Mabon's story are tied to specific place names and may have had individual origin myths of their own. In the order encountered they are described as

- Blackbird of Cilgwri
- Stag of Redynfre
- Owl of Cwm Cowlyd
- Eagle of Gwernabwy
- Salmon of Llyn Llyw

In the *Triads*, Triad 92 lists the 'Three Elders of the World' as 'the Owl of Cwm Cowlyd, the Eagle of Gwernabwy and the Blackbird of Celli Gadarn. The *Irish Book of Lismore* has;

Three life-times of the Stag for the Blackbird
Three life-times of the Blackbird for the Eagle
Three life-times of the Eagle for the Salmon
Three life-times of the Salmon for the Yew

There are also other tales where these animals appear in a similar fashion; one is 'The Ancients of the World' in *The Welsh Fairy Book*, a 1908 collection of folklore. As in *Culhwch and Olwen*, they are consulted to find a specific person or piece of knowledge and again they are poetic in their descriptions of just how ancient they are. In this tale the order of age is slightly different, with the Owl of Cwm Cowlyd being the oldest. There is also another ancient animal listed, the Toad of Cors.

The oldest animals may change with each telling, but clearly the core features of the tale itself are as ancient as the creatures claim to be.

The animals specifically consulted in the search for Mabon have their own significance in Celtic mythology and folklore. Beginning with the blackbird, it is believed that the three birds of Rhiannon from the *Mabinogi* were blackbirds, and that they could sing people into a deathlike sleep. They also feature in *Culhwch and Olwen*, as another of the tasks that Ysbaddaden sets is for the birds of Rhiannon to sing at the wedding feast. Blackbirds tend to sing at dawn and dusk, transitory times often considered to be threshold moments when the Otherworld was easier to access. In some Christian myths the blackbird was considered to herald the Devil, but in the tale of the Irish saint Kevin, a blackbird makes its home upon the saint's hand and even lays an egg there.

The Blackbird of Cilgwri tells Arthur and his men;

When I first came here, there was a smith's anvil here, and I was a young bird. No work has been done on it except by my beak every evening. Today there's not so much of it as a nut that is not worn away.

Then they come to the Stag of Redynfre, who is older still. As mentioned in the last chapter, stags often feature in ancient hunting stories and art. An antlered man, often identified as the god Cernunnos, sits in a lotus position on the Gundestrup Cauldron, a Celtic artifact believed to date back to approx. 100 BC. Holding a snake and a torc, the god or shaman, as he is also identified, seems to be conversing with the animals around him, including a stag. Due to the number of tines on their antlers, the stag is portrayed as older – and therefore wiser – than the seated man. The Irish goddess Flidais was also associated with deer, and in Scotland deer were sometimes referred to as 'fairy cattle.'

The Stag of Redynfre is also no ordinary stag, as he says;

When I first came here, there was only one antler on either side of my head, and there were no trees here except a single oak sapling, and that grew into an oak with a hundred branches. And the oak fell after that, and today nothing remains of it but a red stump. From that day to this I have been here.

The seekers are sent next to the Owl of Cwm Cowlyd, who in other versions of the Celtic 'oldest animals' is the most ancient of the group. Owls have a dual mythology in that they are both wise, ancient birds, yet they are also sometimes seen as representing trickery and deceit, as in the Fourth Branch of the *Mabinogi* where the scheming Blodeuwedd is turned into an owl for betraying Lleu. To hear the call of the owl could be a death omen, and they were also associated with the Cailleach, the ancient Celtic hag goddess or giantess who ruled winter.

The Owl of Cwm Cowlyd is clearly one of the wise, beneficent type, informing the seekers of Mabon that;

When I first came here the large valley that you see was a wooded glen, and a race of men came there and it was destroyed.

42

And the second wood grew in it, and this wood is the third. As
for me, the roots of my wings are mere stumps.

Yet he still has no knowledge of Mabon and so he sends them
to the Eagle of Gwernabwy. Eagles were seen as noble birds,
signifying kingship, and were often regarded as sovereign of
the birds themselves. Lleu transforms into an eagle upon his
attempted murder and this appears to save him from death
until the magician Gwydion is able to turn him back. In *Culhwch*
and Olwen the eagle is the last but one creature that they need
to consult, and he leads the hunting party to the Salmon of Llyn
Lliw with the words;

I came here a long time ago, and when I first came here I had a
rock, and from its top I would peck at the stars every evening.
Now it's not a hands-breadth in sight.

And so only the Salmon of Llyn Lliw is both able to reveal the
location of Mabon's prison and help the men in their rescue
attempt.

It is fitting that only the salmon has this knowledge, as the
Salmon of Wisdom is a common symbol in Celtic myth. In Irish
legend the Salmon of Wisdom lives in the Well of Segais, eating
the magical hazelnuts that fall into it (it is worth noting here
that hazelnuts were a common offering found in the waters of
Chamalieres where Maponus appears to have been venerated).
Salmon appear in much Scottish folklore, including in the tales
of St. Mungo, and they also appear frequently in Pictish art.
They were an important food source in most Northern European
cultures, so their inclusion in myth is perhaps not surprising.

This part of Mabon's tale has an almost aboriginal feel to it,
as the animals recount the ages they have existed, from the

very beginning of time, before the race of men came to the land. They are indelibly a part of the landscape, symbolizing an indigenous wisdom that Arthur and his men are removed from, that is inaccessible to them without the mediation of these ancient creatures. Like the hunting part of the tale, this section feels unmistakably shamanic, taking the reader – or listener – back to a time before civilization, before farming, before men on horseback. And yet in the story Mabon is older still, or simply out of time altogether. Older story threads have linked with newer tales, weaving in, perhaps, folk heroes with local deities and echoes of older spirits of the lands to create what has parallels with a shamanic vision quest.

Modern shamanism is often seen as an important development in current spirituality as it can serve to connect us with the land, animals and the ecological world around us, reminding us that we are part of the ecosystem rather than having dominion over it. To the medieval scribe who wrote down this tale – and its readers – it may have served a similar function, albeit carrying a different meaning than it does today as we face both technological disruption and climate change. The animals represent ages past, a journey back through time and perhaps through the memory of the land itself. Others have suggested that they represent the transmigration of the soul, a type of reincarnation. Caesar stated (using Carey's translation) that the Druids 'foremost tenet' was 'that the soul does not die but crosses over after death from one place to another.'

Practice – Making an Animal Totem

Think about the animals we've discussed so far – the horse, hound, boar/pig, salmon, eagle, blackbird, owl and stag. Does any one animal particularly appeal to you, or is there one you feel a special connection to? Research its myths and attributes, and if the practice appeals to you, try making a totem to bring the wanted attribute into your life – eagle for clarity or foresight, for example.

You can make your totem in any way which appeals to you, but it should be something that can be easily carried in a bag or pocket, or incorporated into jewelry. You don't need to be especially crafty or arty – although if you are, go for it – but your totem will be more personal to you if you make it rather than buy it. You could paint a very simple image onto a stone, for example, or mold a piece of air drying clay into a simple shape and press fur or feathers into it. Once made, hold it in your hand while you meditate on the animal and attributes you've chosen, and then carry it with you.

In the middle of these two ancient mythological motifs – the Oldest Animals and the Wild Hunt – is Mabon himself, imprisoned in his Otherworldly castle, snatched out of time so that even while anvils wear away, oak trees flourish and die, whole forests have their life cycles and mountains wear down, he does not grow old. Let's now examine him as we perhaps know him best; as Exalted Prisoner and Divine Youth.

Chapter 5

The Exalted Prisoner

The first thing that we learn about Mabon – apart from the fact that he is the son of Modron – is his kidnap as a baby and subsequent imprisonment. This theme of Otherworldly imprisonment – often unexplained in the tales that have come down to us – seems to be a common one in the Brythonic stories. We have already looked at how Mabon and Pryderi share a similarity in that they were taken as babies, although Pryderi was adopted by a kindly couple before being returned. Pryderi does, however, experience Otherworldly imprisonment later in life in a mysterious vanishing fortress, along with his mother Rhiannon, and this is a facet of his story that led Gruffyd to suppose a shared seasonal myth that united Pryderi and Mabon.

There are also other divine or semi-divine prisoners who are equated with Mabon. The *Triads* state that there are:

Three Exalted Prisoners in the Land of Britain. Llyr Half-Speech who was imprisoned by Euroswydd, and the second, Mabon son of Modron, and third, Gwair son of Goireioedd. And one who was more Exalted than the three of them, and this Exalted Prisoner was Arthur.

Llyr Half-Speech is a figure whose identity is obscure, but he is considered an ancestral deity, listed as the father in the *Mabinogi* of Bran, Branwen and Manawydan, and sometimes equated with Lir in the Irish myths, as the father of the sea god Manannan mac Lir. Their mother was Penarddun, who subsequently married Euroswydd and had Efnisien and Nisien, also characters in the Second Branch. The tale has been lost, but presumably Llyr is imprisoned so that Euroswydd can marry Penarddun.

Gwair is a more mysterious character. Nothing more is known of him or why he was imprisoned or, indeed, Exalted (this title generally is taken to refer to a deity or legendary hero.) Due to brief mentions in other Welsh texts he has been equated with both Mabon and Pryderi. This equation with Pryderi may come about because of similar sounding names (Pryderi is called Gwri before his kidnap) although Pryderi's father is very clearly Pwyll. He is also mentioned in conjunction with Pryderi in a Taliesin poem known as the *Spoils of Annwfn*, but a quick glance at those lines shows that his imprisonment actually sounds very like that of Mabon's.

Preiddeu Annwfn

In Morus-Baird's 2023 translation, this portion of the poem reads

> *Well-kept was Gwair's prison in Caer Siddi*
> *Throughout the story of Pwyll and Pryderi*
> *Before him no-one had gone there*
> *The heavy, gray chain guarding the best of youths*
> *And he was singing sadly before the spoils of Annwfn*
> *And our poetic prayer shall continue before Doom*

The reference to the 'best of youths' and to him lamenting his imprisonment immediately bring Mabon to mind. There is also the larger story of the *Spoils of Annwfn*, which again features Arthur and his band of warriors. This time, they enter the Otherworld and attempt to steal the Cauldron of Annwfn, and many of them are killed as a result. Morus-Baird believes that the poem indicates that another reason for Arthur and his men to enter Annwfn was to rescue Gwair – just as in *Culhwch and Olwen* they go on a quest to rescue Mabon.

The *Spoils of Annwfn* shares other events with *Culhwch and Olwen*. The cauldron that Arthur and his men attempt to steal from Annwfn is described in the poem as

Kindled by the breath of nine maidens
The cauldron of the Head of Annwfn, what is its disposition
With its dark trim and pearls?
It does not boil a coward's food, it has not been destined to do so.
Lleog's flashing sword was thrust into it
And it was left behind in Lleminog's hand.

In *Culhwch and Olwen,* one of the tasks that Arthur and his men have to accomplish is the stealing of the cauldron of the giant Diwrnach. In order to do so, a character called Llenlleog uses Arthur's sword Caledfwlch (later Excalibur). The Cauldron of Diwrnach is listed in the *Triads* as one of the 'Thirteen Treasures of Britain,' and is described as a cauldron 'which would only boil food for the brave.'

Stressing the similarities between Gwair, Pryderi and Mabon as Otherworldly prisoners to be rescued, Morus-Baird suggests that this is indicative of a shared myth – a basic and older tale of which these different figures are all variants.

There is also a Gware Gwallt Euryn mentioned in *Culhwch and Olwen* who goes with Arthur and Mabon to capture the hounds, who may be equated with Gwair, but also with Pryderi, whose full original name was Gwri Gwallt Euryn. It seems that Gwair is clearly Pryderi, but the description of him in the *Spoils of Annwfn* brings Mabon's myth to mind. Another hint at a shared myth is the nine maidens kindling the cauldron – in the tale of Peredur, he battles nine witches from Caerloyw – the place where Mabon is imprisoned. It seems that at some point all of these tales derived from a single shared myth, of which perhaps Mabon's was the first.

Incarceration and Initiation

Does this suggest, then, that Gruffyd was right about a seasonal myth, a Celtic version of Demeter and Persephone? While it's possible, even probable that the Celts had myths related to the year's turning, given that most ancient peoples sought to explain the changing of the seasons, we don't have anything to indicate that Mabon's imprisonment is analogous to winter, or that his freedom brings spring. Of Gwair we know nothing except that he was imprisoned in Caer Siddi. In Pryderi's tale, however, during his adult imprisonment in the Third Branch, the land of Dyfed does become a type of Wasteland where crops will not grow. This may be an echo of an older seasonal myth, or a myth connected to famines or drought.

There are enough differences in Pryderi and Mabon's stories that it is difficult to tell which aspects are shared and which are not. Also, during Pryderi's brief incarceration, Rhiannon is imprisoned with him, not searching for him as Demeter does. We should bear in mind though – and I go into more detail about this in *Modron* – that the goddess Matrona shares a lot of similarities in her iconography with Demeter, even in name, as the Romans often called her Dea Matrona. But these links are tenuous, and the other shared motifs in these imprisonment tales, of nine women, cauldrons and Otherworldly raids or hunts, take us far away from what might be expected from a simple seasonal myth.

But if Mabon's imprisonment is not about – or at least not just about – winter coming to the land, what is it about? Given its length of time and repeated mentions, there was clearly something significant implied here. It should be remembered also that as *Culhwch and Olwen* wasn't written down until the thirteenth century and appears to be made up of many different parts, original meanings may well have changed. What may have potentially started out as a myth connected to hunting and the famine of winter may have taken on a different significance with the coming of agriculture (which is when myths concerning the lack of crop growth in winter and new growth in spring start to proliferate) and then different meanings again as Britain changed through repeated invasions and the coming of Christianity. The medieval ages themselves, which is when the tales in the *Mabinogi* were first written down, had their own concerns and may have shaped the tales to reflect them. Trying to discover the 'real' or 'true' meaning of Mabon's incarceration may be something of a fruitless search

Scholars can attempt to uncover what it meant to the storytellers telling it, however, and Morus-Baird asks whether the lament of Gwair in the *Spoils of Annwn*, and the lamenting of Mabon, are medieval bardic metaphors for the acquiring of awen, the divine inspiration that every bard seeks. He suggests that the lament of the prisoner is 'a symbol for how the awen arises from the grief of separation between the mortal and immortal realms.' (p243) It is likely that there are bardic metaphors in the tale; it was bards who had to remember – often by the compilation of the *Triads* – and transmit these tales, and Mabon's imprisonment could be seen as a metaphor for a bardic initiation rite, with the Oldest Animals representing the feats of memory needed to remember the various tales and mythological cycles.

Mabon may also have something to do with rebirth and/ or immortality, with the Oldest Animals representing various incarnations. Has Mabon been captured by the Otherworld, unable to reincarnate? A more Christian interpretation could view imprisonment as a dark night of the soul, with Mabon as the Divine Spark, Child or Light, who is eventually rekindled or released. The image of a youth imprisoned out of time, lamenting, is a strangely powerful one that could give rise to many interpretations. Its significance by the time it was written down in *Culhwch and Olwen* is shown by the repeated phrase of 'taken when he was three nights old from between his mother and the wall,' and the stressing of the fact that no-one knows where he is. The salmon of Llyn Llew describes Mabon's lament as a terrible wailing. Mabon himself, when Arthur's men finally find him, tells them;

> *Alas, sir, he who is here has reason to lament. It is Mabon son of Modron who is imprisoned here, and no-one has been so painfully incarcerated in a prison as I, neither the prison of Lludd Llaw Eraint or Graid son of Eri.*

The two other prisoners that Mabon names here are different from the two who are named with him in the *Triads*. Lludd's full name means 'of the silver hand,' which has led to him being associated with the Irish Nuada, believed to be cognate with Nudd and Nodens. He is later listed in the tale as the father of Creiddylad, who is raped by Gwyn ap Nudd although she is engaged to Gwythyr son of Greidol. Because of this, Gwythyr and Gwyn must fight 'every May Day until the Day of Judgment.' This is perhaps an echo of a different seasonal myth, with Gwythyr representing the summer in May, and Gwyn the winter. Certainly many neopagans have interpreted it this way. Graid son of Eri is also mentioned in relation to this tale (which forms a story within a story in *Culhwch and Olwen*) as he fights for Gwythyr and is captured by Gwyn. Graid is also the previous owner of Drudwyn, the dog that Mabon needs to hunt the Twrch Trwyth. As *Culhwch and Olwen* has been described as something of a 'mish-mash' of tales, there are many tangled threads here.

The Arthurian Mabon?

This part of Mabon's myth may also have found its way into the later Arthurian romances, much as his mother Modron has influenced the character of Morgan le Fay and, by association, the Lady of the Lake. The characters of Mabonograin in

Chretien's *Eric and Enid* and Mabuz in *Lanzelet,* by Ulrich von Zatzikhoven, have both been suggested as having been inspired by the story of Mabon.

In *Erec and Enide,* the knight Erec takes part in the enchanted games at the mysterious Court of Joy; games from which no knight returns. The garden is paradisiacal, but there is a stake in the middle which is for his head if he is not successful. He sees a beautiful woman, but is challenged by the ferocious Red Knight when he tries to approach her. Erec defeats the Red Knight, who then tells him that he has been himself imprisoned in the garden, sworn to defend the maiden until a knight defeats him and therefore frees him. The Red Knight reveals that his name is Mabonograin. This doesn't sound very much like Mabon, but Caitlin Matthews (2002) retells a German variant of the myth in which Mabonograin says;

> *There have been no festivals of any kind since I left, because for*
> *all my youth and noble birth, I was buried alive.*

Caitlin Matthews interprets Mabonograin as having 'passed from being a bringer of joy – a role consistent with the Divine Youth, Mabon – into an oppressor of the most restrictive Cronos model. Mabon the youth has become Mabon the titan.' (p191)

In *Lanzelet,* the character of Mabuz is further away still from Mabon's origins. He is the son of the Lady of the Lake (associated with Modron) and he inhabits a Castle of Death – but here he is the jailor, not the jailed, throwing knights into his prison and killing one of them whenever he gets angry.

Myth and Meaning Making

The Exalted Prisoner motif is perhaps the most tangled part of Mabon's myth and without further textual discoveries we are likely to uncover any original myth. It is an interesting exercise to speculate upon, however, for our own personal practice.

What do these shared symbols mean to you? Try meditating on one or a few of those that appeal to you and write down your insights.

The stolen child.
The grieving goddess.
The impregnable fortress.
The imprisoned youth.
The imprisoned youth, lamenting with his harp.
The knights searching for him.
The cauldron. The sword.
The nine witches/muses.

Following this, you might like to write your own version of the Exalted Prisoner – perhaps even as a song, if you are musical. This is not an attempt at an actual historical recreation but rather an exercise of personal gnosis, or spiritual knowledge, exploring what meaning these motifs and tales have for you as an individual.

Who do you identify with in the tale? The stolen child and lamenting prisoner, or the grieving mother goddess? Perhaps the knights who search for him, or the nine women who guard the cauldron? Try writing your tale from these different perspectives.

If you are interested in the bardic interpretations, and the bardic arts in general, you might like to try writing your version of the myth as a poem, or even using the idea of 'imprisonment' as a way to creative inspiration. I'm not suggesting you ask someone to kidnap or imprison you, of course! But in many traditions, a period of withdrawing the senses is believed to inspire creative and/or spiritual knowledge. There are parallels with the idea of the indigenous vision quests, the fasts of monks and nuns, and some old tales that state that druidic Bards would lie under heavy stones in underground caves to achieve inspiration (I'm not suggesting this either; it sounds both uncomfortable and dangerous.) To practice a tamer version, try spending some time in a relatively empty, darkened room where you won't be disturbed. Play some low, rhythmic music or light a candle, and spend time in extended contemplation. See what comes.

In the later Arthurian tales, as in the warrior poems of Owain, Mabon has come far from his roots as a Divine Son of the Mother. It's time to return to them.

Chapter 6

The Divine Youth

It is as the Divine Son, or Youth, that Mabon captured the imagination of the early neo-Druid and neopagan movements. The Order of Bards, Ovates and Druids calls the Winter Solstice 'Alban Arthan' or 'Light of Arthur,' and states;

> *Some Druid orders believe this means the Light of the hero*
> *King Arthur Pendragon who is symbolically reborn as the Sun*
> *Child (the Mabon) at the time of the Solstice.*

As we have seen, nothing about Mabon's myth definitively equates him with the sun, and he is never seen as cognate with King Arthur, but is a much older character with roots in the god Maponos. However, Maponos is equated with Apollo, who was certainly a sun god. Nevertheless, this neo-Druid symbolism is undoubtedly modern, and is intertwined with the idea of Arthur Pendragon as a kind of sleeping Saviour who will return to Britain; a medieval myth which has a clear Christian gloss.

The very name of Divine or Great Son is itself reminiscent of classical pagan sun gods, at least to those interested in comparative mythology. It is often assumed that Christ's birth was celebrated near the Winter Solstice due to his mythic similarities to other deities, many of whom were both sun gods and sons, such as Horus and Mithras. There is also Ovid's *puer aeternus*, or 'eternal youth,' which refers to gods in Classical myths who remain forever young, such as Eros and Iacchus. The *puer aeternus* has also been connected with vegetation gods such as Dionysius, and particularly gods that die and resurrect, such as Tammuz, Attis and Adonis. James Frazer sees a universal myth at work behind all of these figures in his work *The Golden Bough*, which inspired some of the first neopagan groups. W.J. Gruffyd also references these gods as well as Persephone when reading a seasonal myth into the mother and son stories of the *Mabinogi.* Carl Jung saw a Divine Son figure, the *puer aeternus,* as an important archetype, a sort of universal inner child who symbolized the best in humanity; light, innocence and hope for the future. The Divine Son was the archetypal Hero as his younger self, and the son of the Great Mother, the Goddess. In a paper entitled *The Psychology of the Child Archetype,* Jung wrote:

> *The higher and complete man is begotten by an unknown father and born from Wisdom* (often depicted as a goddess) *and it is he who, in the figure of the puer aeternus, represents our totality, which transcends normal consciousness.*

Given these strands, many of which have been important in shaping the neopagan movement as a whole, it is easy to see how Mabon has also been viewed in this vein. Yet, despite some similarities and a shared Indo-European root, Classical and Celtic myth is not so easily compared, and there is a great deal of difference as well as similarity. To simply label Mabon as another reflex of a universal *puer aeternus* figure, or a stage in the life of the legendary hero Arthur, is to obscure his origins in both myth and culture (as well as the Welsh origins of Arthur himself.) Such 'universal' archetypes, as pointed out by critical scholars including feminists, tend to be not universal at all but largely concerned with the experience of men, and particularly of white, Western men who are well-off, able-bodied and straight. As I hope I have shown in the previous chapters, there are many different layers to the tale of Mabon and still much left to be uncovered, both in terms of scholarship and personal spiritual/religious practice.

There are other examples of Divine Youths in Celtic myth, and we shall look at these in this chapter, and what relation they may have with Mabon. We have already seen how Mabon is considered to be reflected in the other sons of the *Mabinogi*, most prominently Pryderi, and at his relationship with Owain son of Urien. In this chapter, we will look briefly again at Taliesin, and more closely at the Irish Aengus mac Og.

Taliesin as Divine Youth

We've already met Taliesin, thanks to his shamanic sounding poetry and the fact that he is one of the few people outside of the scribes of *Culhwch and Olwen* to mention Mabon, but in many ways the bard has become something of a mystical divine youth figure himself. Although many scholars dismiss his origin story as a 'Tudor folk tale' (Williams, 2021) rather than a genuine remnant of ancient mythology, there is no denying that the themes of his tale reflect those we see in other stories, including those of the *Mabinogi*, and he himself is mentioned within those tales as being an honored bard of the royal court. Reborn from the womb of the witch Cerridwen (who has become a neopagan deity in her own right, just like the women in the *Mabinogi* tales) after stealing the magical drops of awen from her cauldron and shapeshifting into various forms to get away from her, Taliesin is cast as a baby into the ocean. From the moment he is found, it is clear that he is a very special child. His name means 'shining brow.'

As well as mentioning the warrior Mabon and using the title to refer to Christ, Taliesin refers to himself as a Mabon or divine figure in some of his poetry. In *The Battle of the Trees*, he describes himself as

...formed.
Of the flower of nettles,
Of the water of the ninth wave.

I was enchanted by Math,
Before I became immortal,
I was enchanted by Gwydion
The great purifier of the Brython,
Of Eurwys, of Euron,
Of Euron, of Modron.

Here Taliesin seems to be referencing the Fourth Branch of the *Mabinogi*, equating himself to a figure like Blodeuwedd, who is made from flowers and enchanted by the magician Gwydion, as well as being immortal. But note, too, how he also includes Modron as one of his creators, likening himself to the Divine Son, Mabon. Like the *Spoils*, the *Battle* is an obscure text that has been puzzling readers for centuries, and so it's likely that another piece of myth around Modron and potentially Mabon is being referred to here, that we just don't currently have enough existing information to decipher.

The stories surrounding Taliesin don't stop at his miraculous birth and rescue; he is also described as being imprisoned (just like Gweir and Mabon) and tested by the goddess Arianrhod. Only by going through these trials does he obtain his full bardic skills. This offers another hint that the trials of the Exalted Prisoner may have been an allegory for initiation, or had become so by the medieval period..

Whoever the historical Taliesin may have been, the mythology that has sprung up around him seems to have absorbed earlier tales which may include those of Mabon himself. Mabon is sometimes described by neopagan sources as a god of music and/or poetry, and we know that Maponus himself was depicted with a lyre.

Aengus mac Og

What about the Goidelic sources? While academics caution against viewing Irish and Scottish deities and myth as exactly cognate with those of the Brythonic tradition, there are often undeniable similarities which are interesting to examine. 'Mabon' becomes 'mac og' in old Gaelic and the Irish deity Aengus mac Og has some fascinating parallels with Mabon, although his known mythos is much richer.

Aengus is also a divine youth, but he is the son of a god (the father god the Dagda) as well as a river goddess, this time the goddess Boann of the river Boyne. He made his home at Bru na Boinne, a Neolithic ritual complex in County Meath that is complete with standing stones, burial mounds and an association with the Winter Solstice. Boann is married to Elcmar, but has an affair with the Dagda, who 'makes the sun stand still' to deceive Elcmar while Boann gives birth to Aengus, who later takes over the Bru na Boinne from his father the Dagda (or in some versions the Dagda helps him take it from Elcmar). This tale is often viewed as a myth concerning the Winter Solstice, with Aengus being the son/sun that is reborn.

Also a shamanic and bardic figure, Aengus was also associated with shapeshifting, music and poetry. Unlike Mabon, however, he is a god of love rather than of the hunt, although he is also sometimes depicted as a warrior of the Tuatha de Danann, riding a white horse and wielding a sword known as the Great Fury. He is known in Scotland as Angus, husband of the maiden goddess Bride, and later folktales (Mackenzie, 1917) refer to him as 'mounting his white steed and riding Eastward... clad in shining gold' and a folk song depicts him as

Angus hath come – the young the fair,
The blue-eyed god with golden hair.

In perhaps the most famous story which features Aengus, *The Wooing of Etain,* he, like Mabon in *Culhwch and Olwen,* is not the hero but rather an important helper, who helps the hero get the girl. In most translations, Aengus is referred to often simply as 'Mac Oc/Og.'

He also plays a helper/mentor role in the tale *Diarmuid and Grainne*, but in this story Aengus is a father rather than a son. As foster father of Diarmuid, he tries to help him escape with Grainne from the legendary Fionn by hiding Grainne under his invisible cloak (which makes him into a wizard character) and later, when Diarmuid is killed, Aengus grieves and takes his body to Bru na Boinne. In a twist on the Welsh tale of Mabon, Diarmuid is killed in a boar hunt engineered by Fionn (often seen as an 'Irish Arthur.')

Let's recap what we know so far about Mabon himself, as a distinct and separate figure. To summarize, Maponos was a Celtic god associated with a healing spring at Chamalieres, who also had an association with the Otherworld, and was called upon to mediate with Otherworld spirits for healing. In our earliest knowledge of him he was a healing and water god, perhaps originally a local nature spirit associated with a particular spring. He is believed to be associated with the river goddess Matrona, largely due to their names and associations with water and healing.

Maponus is also found in the North of what is now England and the South of what is now Scotland, and there seems to have been a large area dedicated to his cult there, attested to by place names and inscriptions, found mostly along Hadrian's Wall, where there is also found reliefs of the Matronae. His iconography here links him with dogs, hunting and harps, and the Romans twinned him with the god Apollo.

In Taliesin's earlier poems, Mabon turns up as a warrior from the North, possibly equated with Owain, son of Urien. Urien, a King in the North, has Owain with Modron, who is cognate with Matrona. Mabon's only surviving myth comes to us from *Culhwch and Olwen* in the *Mabinogi*, where he is revealed as the son of Modron who was stolen from her as a baby. He was imprisoned in an Otherworldly fortress, which can be found at the banks of the River Severn in Gloucester, where he stayed for millennia as a youth, lamenting.

Arthur's men free him with the help of the Oldest Animals, give him an Otherworldly horse and hound, and he joins the hunt of the Twrch Trwyth as an Otherworldly huntsman, and takes the magical razor from between the boars' ears. This is a story which has older, shamanic echoes, as well as likely containing references to medieval bardic practice.

In later Arthurian tales his story influenced the characters of Mabonograin and Mabuz. Only much later, in the twentieth century, does he become explicitly venerated as a sun god born at the Winter Solstice, or have his name used for the Autumn Equinox.

For feminists and those looking to break away from the traditional gender divides we find in both ancient myths and tales and, sadly, some of the neopagan movement itself, Mabon and his tales may offer another mystery. We have seen how his most well-known title is about his maternity. He is the 'son of Modron,' before he is anything else, and his stealing away from his mother is repeated over and over by the Oldest Animals. The four branches of the *Mabinogi* are explicitly concerned with mothers and sons and more specifically, mothers who for one reason or another lose their sons, either temporarily or permanently. We know this by now, but what is often overlooked is why this was considered such an important motif. While most scholars have looked for archetypal significance or seasonal myth, others have looked at the sociological causes, pointing out that in medieval times children often died, and the sons of elite women were often fostered out, causing mothers and sons to indeed be separated. But would medieval storytellers and bards, who were nearly always male, have thought this significant?

This consideration has led some to suggest that the Four Branches were written down by a woman; specifically Gwenllian, a princess of Wales.

As well as a focus on the plight of mothers who lost their sons, the first four tales differ from the others in important ways. Rather than glorifying patriarchal heroes and their exploits, as tales such as Culhwch and Olwen seem to, the stories of Rhiannon and Pryderi, Branwen, and Arianrhod and Lleu seem to offer caution and criticism. This is a topic for a bigger work than this little book, but it is certainly something to think about when we consider these tales, as well as the enduring importance of Mabon and Modron. What is it they are trying to tell us today? I will briefly offer some of my own thoughts in the Afterword.

As there are so many strands to his history and character, with so many mysteries remaining as to his origins and his full original mythos, Mabon turns out to be more complex than a quick Google search would reveal. The best way to get to know him as a practitioner (depending on your belief system) is to work with him, and to build a relationship.

Chapter 7

Working with Mabon

Before we look at ritual or invocation, it's time to address the question that often has pagans and academics alike locked in heated debates online every September. Is Mabon the pagan name for the Autumn Equinox?

To say anything but yes might seem like nit-picking, considering that as far as many of today's practitioners are considered, that is the name they use and have always used. But as we become more aware of both misinformation and cultural appropriation in spiritual circles, this is a debate which is likely to rage for some time.

Although the figure of Mabon in his current form may be, by the most conservative estimate, at least seven hundred years old, the use of his name for the Autumn Equinox didn't occur until the 1970's when prominent neopagan Aidan Kelly very deliberately gave it this title. In a blog post, Kelly explains his reasoning;

We have Gaelic names for the four Celtic holidays. It offended my aesthetic sensibilities that there seemed to be no Pagan names for the summer solstice or the fall equinox ... so I decided to supply them ... the Eleusinian mysteries, which were the actual religion of Greece, began at the full moon nearest the Equinox...I began looking for a similar sort of myth in northern Europe. I could not find one in Germanic or Gaelic literature, but there was one in the Welsh, in the Mabinogion collection, the story of Mabon ap Modron (which translates as "Son of the Mother," just as Kore simply meant "girl") ... so I picked "Mabon" as the name for the holiday in my calendar. It was not an arbitrary choice. I sent a copy of the calendar to

Oberon (then still Tim), who liked these new names and began using them in Green Egg, whence they passed into the national Pagan vocabulary.

Kelly based his choice on a similar theory to Gruffyd's, of there being a similarity or even mythic link between the stories of Demeter and Kore/Persephone and that of Modron and Mabon. As discussed above, it isn't impossible, but there is also no real evidence that this is the case. And while, as I've said, Matrona has been seen by some as a Celtic Demeter, due to her iconography of fruits and loaves and full cornucopias, by the time of the Welsh myths Modron has no such associations. Rather, Modron seems to have come full circle as a river goddess and then enters Arthurian tradition, potentially inspiring the character of Morgan le Fay. And neither the older Maponus nor Mabon have any known association with either autumn or the harvest. While the motifs of separation and imprisonment do suggest an underlying seasonal myth, there is nothing other than the shared motif of a stolen child to link Mabon with Persephone and her seasonal rites.

Honoring Mabon at the Autumn Equinox then is a practitioner's personal choice, and a perfectly valid one, but this is different to literally naming a festival after a deity that was likely never honored in that way. It is just as valid, for example, to use those motifs of separation and imprisonment, of Divine Mother and Divine Son, to honor Mabon at Yule, as many modern Druids have a tendency to do. There is a little more precedent for this, given that Maponus was twinned with the Hyperborean Apollo who as a sun god disappears in the darkest month and then returns, but Maponos himself seems to have originated as the deity of a local spring, and Mabon is never associated with the sun.

It seems to me that Samhain would be a more appropriate time to honor Mabon, given his actual associations with the hunt and the Otherworld. Or even Spring, as he is a youth associated with water and healing springs. To name the Autumn Equinox (not an actual Celtic festival) after him does seem somewhat arbitrary, despite Aidan Kelly's protestations.

Of course, Kelly could not have realized how much his naming system would catch on, and that perhaps is the real problem here. For, rather than being a matter of personal choice, a tradition out of many neopagan traditions, Mabon as an Equinox harvest festival has gone global (although it seems to be most popular in the US) and many practitioners are likely to not know the origins of the name or when and why it became attached to the festival.

Typing 'Mabon' into Google reveals a host of images of autumn leaves, corn, bread, apples and pomegranates, followed by a plethora of high traffic websites and blogs referring to the 'pagan Thanksgiving' and saying things such as 'In ancient times Mabon was the second harvest festival' or 'Ancient Celts and pagans used this day to give thanks to nature for a good harvest.' There is even a tarot deck by a popular author dedicated to the 'season of Mabon,' which is designed to 'give thanks for the abundance of Mother Earth.'

Myths do change over time, and it tends to be the myths and stories that can adapt that are preserved. But what has happened with Mabon is not the organic adaptation of a myth so much as the taking of his name, shorn of his story and actual associations, entirely out of context.

The problem with all this is the obscuring of a genuine mythical tradition and the appropriation of Welsh culture and language. Many Welsh pagans find this continuing appropriation offensive and it must be beyond frustrating to have to keep countering such a flood of misinformation.

Unfortunately, given its growth and popularity, the festival of Mabon probably isn't going anywhere. What we can do is examine our own practices and be mindful of the ongoing issues. If you're a reader who genuinely thought Mabon was simply a harvest festival until picking up this book, then this section has hopefully given you some food for thought!

What follows in this chapter are suggestions for associations and for ritual to call upon Mabon – as archetype, metaphor or deity, depending on your own practice – for sure-footed guidance, healing and inspiration, in keeping with the attributes we've been looking at in the previous chapters. These are simply suggestions and examples, based on my own research practices, so feel free to adapt or discard as you please. I've also given an example below of an invocation that could be used to call upon Mabon, which includes references to most of the seasons. As you read it, see what images and ideas resonate with you, and think about where you would personally place Mabon in the Wheel of the Year. Then, you might like to try writing your own invocation.

Invocation to Mabon
I am the stag of the wild greenwood,
The rustle in the golden autumn leaves.
I am the whisper in the morning breeze,
The seeker in the evening's amber glow

I am the light in the heart of the apple,
The wisdom in the silent, ancient stones.
I am the shadow in the fading summer,
The promise in the seeds that wait to grow

I am the hound, fleet-footed and wise,
Tracking the mysteries under the moonlit skies.
I am the hunter, silent and sure,
Guiding the arrow with intent pure

I am the healer, hands gentle and kind,
Mending the broken, the lost I find.
I am the bard, voice weaving the tale,
In song and story, let truth prevail

I call upon you, Mabon, child of light,
Keeper of the balance, fading bright.
In the twilight of the year, hear my voice,
Guide us through the dark, grant us your choice

Grant us your wisdom, O son of Modron,
In the turning of the year, in the waning sun.
Bless us with bounty, with balance restore,
Mabon, in your honor, we forever endure

I am the lantern in the dark of Samhain,
The keeper of the veil, the end and begin.
I am the spark in the heart of Yule,
The fire reborn, the light renewed

I am the promise in the snowdrop's bloom,
Whispering of the spring, dispelling gloom.
I am the laughter in the lengthening days,
The warmth returning, the sun's gentle rays

I call upon you, Mabon, child of light,
Keeper of the balance, fading bright.
In the twilight of the year, hear my voice,
Guide us through the dark, grant us your choice

Grant us your wisdom, O son of Modron,
Through the cycle of seasons, under sun and moon.
Bless us with bounty, with balance restore,
Mabon, in your honor, we forever endure

Associations and Altars

A big part of much neopagan practice is ritual, which often involves special objects and an altar. Below I've given examples, drawn from the information we've been discussing, of colors, animals, correspondences, crystals and herbs that might resonate for working with Mabon. If any of these don't feel right to you, use your own.

- Animal – Horse, hound, boar/pig, salmon.
- Color – Blue, brown, white.
- Correspondences – Music, poetry, hunting, healing.
- Crystals – Quartz, jasper, petrified wood. (Please, at the risk of sounding preachy, source your crystals ethically. Or if this is expensive, use simple stones that you find while out and about. This is a practice I love and is great to do with kids, too.)
- Elements – Water (especially rivers and springs).
- Herbs/plants – Lavender and nettle.
- Moon phases – New and full.
- Oils – Cinnamon, cedar, lavender, pine.
- Spellworkings – Trance journeying, healing, achieving goals, creative inspiration.
- Symbols – The hunt, fortresses, the harp/lyre, anything associated with horses or dogs.

Altars are very individual to each person and can be simple or elaborate, temporary or permanent, so be guided by your own intuition here. If you would like an example, my altar to Mabon consisted of

- A bowl of spring water.
- A horseshoe.
- A statue of a dog.
- A wooden sculpture of a mother and child.

- A large piece of clear quartz.
- Blue and white candles.

Ritual for Liberation

Creating a ritual to invoke Mabon during a full moon, focusing on liberation from something that is holding you back, can be a powerful spiritual practice. Here's a suggested approach for such a ritual.

Choose a quiet, comfortable spot where you can see the moon. Lay out your altar cloth and arrange your materials on it. These should include something to represent a hound, a small bowl of salt water and a salt dish, paper and pen, patchouli or sandalwood incense, black and white candles and any offerings, such as fruit and wine. I find apples and ale a good choice for working with Mabon in this way.

Cleanse the space by smudging with incense or sprinkling with the salt water. Visualize a circle of protective energy around your space, saying something like:

I cast this circle to create a sacred space, free from outside influences.

Light the candles on your altar and the incense if you haven't already. Invoke Mabon by reciting the tailored invocation, focusing on his aspects as a liberated deity and guide through transitions.

Mabon, son of Modron, as the full moon shines above, I call upon your wisdom and strength. Guide me in breaking free from what binds me, as the hunter pursues freedom in the wildwood, and the hound seeks out hidden paths.

Write down what you wish to be freed from on the paper.

Meditate on this issue, visualizing it as a tangible chain or rope binding you.

Then, either tear the paper into small pieces or safely burn it (if possible), symbolizing your release from these bonds.

As you do this, say:

Under the full moon's light, I release these bonds. With Mabon's guidance, I break free and step forward into new beginnings.

Place your seasonal fruits on the altar as an offering to Mabon. Pour a libation (cider or wine) onto the earth (or into a bowl if indoors) as a gesture of gratitude. Visualize the circle of energy dissipating and say:

The circle is open, but unbroken. May the liberation of Mabon remain in my heart.

Ground yourself by eating a small snack or simply sitting and breathing deeply for a few minutes.

Clean up your space, ensuring any fire is completely extinguished.

A Ritual for Hunting Down Your Goals

As before, choose a quiet place where you can focus without interruptions. Set up your space and cast your circle in whichever way you prefer, or you can repeat the simple routine given in the ritual above.

Light your candles while focusing on the specific goals they represent. Visualize each goal as a flame being ignited. Stand before your altar and say:

Mabon, master of the hunt, guide of the focused arrow, I invoke your presence. Lend me your determination and clarity, so that I may achieve my goals with precision and success. As the hunter pursues their quarry with skill and patience, so too shall I pursue my aspirations. Mabon, be with me.

Write down your goals clearly and concisely on the paper. Read each goal aloud, visualizing yourself achieving them. Place the paper in the bowl or cauldron.

Hold your hands over the bowl/cauldron and imagine a bright light (the color of your chosen candles) emanating from your hands, infusing your written goals with energy. Say:

With Mabon's guidance, these goals I set will manifest. I am the hunter; my intentions are my arrows, true and swift.

Give thanks to Mabon for his presence and support. Make any libations. Keep the cauldron on your altar while you pursue your goals.

As before, close and ground.

Healing Ritual

In preparation for a healing ritual invoking Maponus, ensure you have a clean and sacred space set up, perhaps adorned with an altar cloth in soothing colors like blue or green. Light candles representing healing energy and place a bowl or chalice of spring water on the altar, symbolizing purity and renewal.

Gather a symbolic representation of the body part that requires healing, such as a drawing, figurine, or picture.

Begin by centering yourself in front of the altar. Take several deep breaths to ground yourself and focus your energy. As you light the candles, visualize the presence of healing energy surrounding you, filling the space with warmth and light. With a sense of sincerity and reverence, invoke Maponus, addressing him as the divine healer whose gentle touch brings comfort and renewal. Call upon his guidance in this sacred space, seeking his healing light to flow through you.

Hold the symbolic representation of the body part in need of healing in your hands. Envision healing energy surrounding it, filling it with warmth and light. Place the representation on the altar, facing the candles, as a focal point for the healing energies. Bless the spring water by holding the chalice or bowl in your hands, and infuse it with your intention for healing. Speak a blessing over the water, asking for it to carry the energy of renewal and restoration.

Dip your fingertips into the blessed spring water and gently anoint the symbolic representation of the body part, tracing small circles or symbols. Focus your intentions on healing, visualizing the body part becoming whole and healthy. Express gratitude to Maponus for his presence and assistance in the healing ritual. You may extinguish the candles, if desired, or let them burn safely. Close the ritual space by thanking any spirits or energies you called upon and releasing them.

As a reminder of your healing intentions, keep the representation of the body part on your altar or in a prominent place. Consider drinking the blessed spring water or using it in a bath for further healing and purification.

A Ritual for Creative Inspiration

Prepare your space by cleansing it with smudging or incense, clearing away any stagnant energy that might inhibit creativity.

Set up your altar with a vibrant cloth and light candles in colors like gold, yellow, or orange, symbolizing the presence of creative energy. Before the altar, take a moment to center yourself, grounding your energy and focusing your intention on invoking Maponus/Mabon, the deity of the creative spirit. Speak a heartfelt invocation, acknowledging him as a patron of the arts and a source of inspiration. Invite him into the sacred space, asking for his guidance in unlocking your creative potential.

Reflect on your creative goals and aspirations, writing them down in your journal or on a piece of paper. Visualize yourself fully immersed in your creative pursuits, feeling the joy and fulfillment that comes with artistic expression. Offer symbols of creativity on your altar, such as paintbrushes, musical instruments, or images of artwork, as a gesture of reverence. Additionally, offer a small portion of food or drink to honor the god and express gratitude for his inspiration.

Engage in a creative activity that resonates with you. Whether it's painting, writing, playing music, or any other form of artistic expression, allow yourself to flow with the creative energy, letting inspiration guide your actions. As you create, feel the presence of Mabon/Maponus infusing your work with his muse-like energy, guiding your hands and mind in the pursuit of artistic expression and innovation.

Once you have finished your creative endeavor, take a moment to express gratitude to Mabon/Maponus for his presence and inspiration in the ritual. You may extinguish the candles, if desired, or let them burn safely. Close the ritual space by thanking any spirits or energies you called upon and releasing them. Take time to reflect on your creative experience, jotting down any insights or ideas that emerged during the ritual. Keep the symbols of creativity on your altar as a reminder of your connection to this god of inspiration.

Afterword

A Wilder Sacred Masculine

I am aware that, by mentioning a concept such as the 'sacred masculine,' I risk universalising Mabon into a generic archetype, something that I earlier cautioned against. But, while appreciating Mabon as a specific, cultural figure with his own history, I believe we can still talk about what he may have to teach us in terms of how we think about gender norms, mythology and how we live in the world. What follows are my own personal reflections which you may or may not agree with, but I hope they encourage you to think about some of these things yourself.

Western civilization has, historically, loved the myth of the 'Hero's Journey,' a Western male who goes on a quest, slays the monster and restores order. The peoples we now refer to as Celtic were no exception and their tribal cultures were often warlike. The medieval bards, including Taliesin, spent much of their time singing praises to kings and warriors and glorifying slaughter on the battlefield. Many of the Arthurian tales are typical heroes' journeys, and the full tale of *Culhwch and Olwen* has some aspects of this, as well as parts that are brutal and violent. Taliesin portrays Mabon himself as a bloodthirsty warrior on a magnificent steed, who none could stand against.

I don't like these stories. Most neopagans today, as far as I can tell, who express an enthusiasm for 'Celtic' spirituality are thinking more about values of connectedness with nature, cyclical time, hospitality and perhaps making contact with the Otherworld; than they are about war and battle and destroying other tribes. Nevertheless we still often celebrate these tales, re-interpreting them so they are about bravery and valor, and the 'Hero's Journey' becomes a metaphor for our own personal growth. Nothing wrong with that, but I also think that some of these tales, especially those such as Mabon, with their hints at older cultural themes, have a different vision to offer us. The first four tales of the *Mabinogi*, for example, known as the Four Branches, while still retaining many aspects of heroic journeys, also subvert these tropes and show the pitfalls of power, greed and violence, especially for women and children and those who are not ideal heroes.

And what about Mabon himself? As I stated earlier, in *Culhwch and Olwen* he is not the hero. He is, first and foremost, the son of a mother. He is a youth who sings. Who cries, even. He is a shamanic figure, lord of the hunt, the horse and the hound. Once he has taken what he needs from the boar, he seems to leave. He isn't there when the boar is driven into the sea or killed. He isn't a warrior or a killer. In fact, he needs rescuing from his long exile and imprisonment. In his earlier guise as Maponus he seems to have been predominantly a son, a shamanic healer, a hunter/houndlord and a musician or bard. Likely, in his very first murmurings, a local healing spirit of a bubbling spring.

His story offers us an antidote to the warrior and the lone hero. The energy I personally get from Mabon is wild, but regenerative. Life-giving rather than death-dealing. And although I have used the term 'Sacred Masculine' I think the term itself needs rewilding. These stories, these energies, aren't confined to men or those who are gendered male. In her book on sacred masculinity, *The Flowering Wand*, Sophie Strand explores our myths of male gods and asks for a more genderfluid, ecologically connected vision. A collective journey that is about healing the whole community, rather than striving for personal glory.

I agree with her. I believe that, for those of us who practice a Celtic/Brythonic spirituality, Mabon can help to offer us this. For me, today, that's what his story is about.

It's about time we let him return from his long exile, let him help us rewild ourselves and our youth, and learn to tell new stories and sing new songs.

References

Aldhouse-Green, Miranda *Sacred Britannia; The Gods and Rituals of Roman Britain* (2023) Thames and Hudson

BanDea, Kelle *Modron; Meeting the Celtic Mother Goddess* (2024) Pagan Portals, Moon Books

Baring-Gould, Sabine *Lives of the Saints* (1898) reprinted 2009 by Cornell University Library

Bath, Michael *Donne's Anatomy of the World and the Legend of the Oldest Animals* (1981) *The Review of English Studies* Vol 32 Number 127 pp302-308 https://www.jstor.org/stable/515167 accessed 12/11/23

Berezkin, Yuri *Cosmic Hunt; Variants of Siberian-North American Myth* (2005) *Folklore* Vol 31 https://www.researchgate.net/publication/26484663_Cosmic_Hunt_Variants_of_Siberian-North_American_Myth accessed 14/11/2023

Bromwich, Rachel (ed) *Trioedd Ynys Prydein: The Triads of the Island of Britain* (2006) University of Wales Press

Carey, John (trans) and Koch, John T (ed) *The Celtic Heroic Age; Literary Sources for Ancient Celtic Europe and Early Ireland and Wales* (2003) Celtic Studies Publications

Child, Francis James, in Lang, Andrew (ed) *The English and Scottish Popular Ballads, Vol 1 of 5: The Child Ballads* (2007) Forgotten Books

Coneller, Chantal *Technological Analysis of the World's Earliest Shamanic Costume* (2016) Plos One https://journals.plos.org/plosone/article?id=10.1371/journal.pone.0152136 accessed 14/11/2023

Davies, Sioned (ed) *The Mabinogion* (2007) Oxford World Classics

Gerald of Wales, O'Meara, John (trans) *The History and Topography of Ireland* (1982) Penguin Classics

Gruffyd, William John *Rhiannon; An Inquiry into the Origin of the First and Third Branches of the Mabinogi* (1953) reprinted 2021 Hassel St Press

Haussler, Ralph *Apollo Cunomaglos, Lord of the Wolves* (2018) *Bandue: Revista de la Sociedad Española de Ciencias de las Religiones* Vol 11 0065-82

Hull, Eleanor *The Hawk of Achill or the Legend of the Oldest Animals* (1932) *Folklore* Vol43 Number 4 pp 376-409 https://www.jstor.org/stable/1256264 accessed 12/11/23

Jung, C.G. *The Psychology of the Child Archetype* in *The Collected Works of CG Jung* (1945) Princeton University Press

Kaliff, Anders and Terje, Oestigaard *The Great Indo-European Horse Sacrifice; 4000 Years of Cosmological Continuity from Sintashta and the Steppe to Scandinavian Skeid.* (2020) Uppsala University

Kelly, Aidan *About Naming Ostara, Litha and Mabon* Patheos Pagan (2017) https://www.patheos.com/blogs/aidankelly/2017/05/naming-ostara-litha-mabon/ accessed 19/12/23

Lecouteux, Claude *Phantom Armies of the Night; The Wild Hunt and the Ghostly Processions of the Undead* (2011) Inner Traditions

Lewis, Gwyneth and Williams, Rowan *The Book of Taliesin; Poems of Warfare and Praise in an Enchanted Britain* (2019) Penguin Classics

Ludbrook, Kim Shamanism: what you need to know about the fastest-growing 'religion' in England and Wales (5th January 2023) The Conversation https://theconversation.com/shamanism-what-you-need-to-know-about-the-fastest-growing-religion-in-england-and-wales-196438#:~:text=Just%20650%20people%20said%20they,countries'%20fastest%2Dgrowing%20religion accessed 23/12/23

Matthews, Caitlin *Mabon and the Guardians of Celtic Britain; Hero Myths in the Mabinogion* (2002) Inner Traditions

Matthews, Caitlin and Matthews, John *The Lost Book of the Grail: The Sevenfold path of the Grail and the Restoration of the Faery Accord* (2019) Inner Traditions

Matthews, John *Taliesin: The Last Celtic Shaman* (2002) Inner Traditions

Mackenzie, Donald Alexander *Wonder Tales from Scottish Myth and Legend* (1917) Frederick A Stokes, Co.

Morus-Baird, Dr Gwilym *Taliesin Origins; Exploring the Myth of the Greatest Celtic Bard* (2023) Celtic Source

Order of Bards, Ovates and Druids *Winter Solstice – Alban Arthan* (2023) https://druidry.org/druid-way/teaching-and-practice/druid-festivals/winter-solstice-alban-arthan accessed 23/12/23

Strand, Sophie *The Flowering Wand; Rewilding the Sacred Masculine – Lunar Kings, Trans-species Magicians and Rhizomatic Harpists* (2022) Inner Traditions

Telyndru, Jhenah *The Ninefold Way of Avalon; Walking the Path of the Priestess* (2023) Llewellyn Publications

Thomas, W. Jenkyn *The Welsh Fairy Book* (1908) New York, F.A. Stokes

Young, William A *Ghosts of the Forest; The Lost Mythology of the North* (2022) inter-celtic

MS Peniarth 1 can be found online at the National Library of Wales https://www.library.wales/

Recommended Resources

As well as the above references, for those who wish to go deeper on any of the research or ideas discussed in *Mabon*, but prefer videos, blogs or online courses to a stack of books, I recommend the following, as I have found their research and work to be invaluable:

Dr. Gwilym Morus-Baird's work at Celtic Source, especially his course on the Native Tales, including *Culhwch and Olwen* https://celticsource.online/

Kris Hughes at Go Deeper https://www.godeeper.info/

Bestsellers from Moon Books

Keeping Her Keys
An Introduction to Hekate's Modern Witchcraft
Cyndi Brannen
*Blending Hekate, witchcraft and personal development
together to create a powerful new magickal perspective.*
Paperback: 978-1-78904-075-3 ebook 978-1-78904-076-0

Journey to the Dark Goddess
How to Return to Your Soul
Jane Meredith
*Discover the powerful secrets of the Dark Goddess
and transform your depression, grief and pain
into healing and integration.*
Paperback: 978-1-84694-677-6 ebook: 978-1-78099-223-5

Shamanic Reiki
Expanded Ways of Working with Universal Life Force Energy
Llyn Roberts, Robert Levy
*Shamanism and Reiki are each powerful ways of healing; together,
their power multiplies. Shamanic Reiki introduces techniques to
help healers and Reiki practitioners tap ancient healing wisdom.*
Paperback: 978-1-84694-037-8 ebook: 978-1-84694-650-9

Southern Cunning
Folkloric Witchcraft in the American South
Aaron Oberon
*Modern witchcraft with a Southern flair, this book is a
journey through the folklore of the American South and
a look at the power these stories hold for modern witches.*
Paperback: 978-1-78904-196-5 ebook: 978-1-78904-197-2

Readers of ebooks can buy or view any of these bestsellers by clicking on the live link in the title. Most titles are published in paperback and as an ebook. Paperbacks are available in traditional bookshops. Both print and ebook formats are available online.

Find more titles and sign up to our readers' newsletter
www.collectiveinkbooks.com/paganism

For video content, author interviews and more, please subscribe to our YouTube channel.

MoonBooksPublishing

Follow us on social media for book news, promotions and more:

Facebook: Moon Books

Instagram: @MoonBooksCI

X: @MoonBooksCI

TikTok: @MoonBooksCI